D0068480

ONE LIFE

WHAT'S IT ALL ABOUT?

RICO TICE | BARRY COOPER

One Life. What's it All About?
Copyright © 2017 Christianity Explored
www.christianityexplored.org
First published as Christianity Explored in 2002.
This edition published 2017. Reprinted 2021.

Published by:
The Good Book Company

thegoodbook.com | thegoodbook.co.uk
thegoodbook.com.au | thegoodbook.co.nz | thegoodbook.co.in

ISBN: 9781784982508 | Printed in India

Design by André Parker

CONTENTS

For Valerie Cooper
and Catherine Tice
who loved us unconditionally

1.
IT'S JUST GOOD NEWS

First of all, I have a confession to make.

There is another book that has been around a lot longer than this one, and it has exactly the same aim: to make you familiar with who Jesus Christ was and why he is of absolute importance to everyone who has ever lived and ever will live.

The person behind this other book is infinitely more gifted than I am, and the book's scope is admittedly superior to the one you're currently holding. Copies are readily available not only on the internet, in book stores and in libraries, but also in hotel rooms the world over, and it is so popular that parts of it have been translated into over 2,500 languages.

Actually, I'd better make that two confessions. The second is that I didn't have a particularly religious upbringing myself. In fact, my experience of Christianity was limited to a few dull sermons, slightly spooky people in strange garments hanging about in dank halls and religious education lessons during which I attempted to find references to rugby in the Bible.

Christianity was worse than boring: it was a fiction. Jesus walking on water, the three wise men, the feeding of the five thousand, Father Christmas and Winnie the Pooh were all mixed up in my mind together. They were all make-believe, best left in the nursery.

So I was shocked when I discovered that my older brother George had become a Christian. I remember telling him in no uncertain terms exactly what I thought about God and everything connected with God. To his credit, George didn't respond in kind. Instead, he pointed me to a single sentence in the Bible, the very first sentence of Mark chapter 1:

The beginning of the gospel about Jesus Christ...

He explained that the word "gospel" simply means "good news". "Rico," he said, "you don't understand Christianity. You think it's all about church, men in dresses, obeying rules and beautiful old buildings, but it's not. It's just good news. Good news about Jesus Christ."

Even my time in church, however, had brought me no closer to knowing what this "good news about Jesus Christ" actually was. In fact, if I could hand the book you're now holding to the person I was thirty-odd years ago, that person would have dismissed it straight away.

He wouldn't even have given it the benefit of the doubt, which is strange because – as I've since discovered – Jesus Christ is able to provide satisfying answers to questions that were endlessly troubling to me. How can I be content? Is there any meaning to life? Is there life after death? Does God really exist or did we just make him up ourselves? If God exists, why is the world so full of injustice?

I suppose most of us already have an opinion about God.

Some people look at the world, with all its suffering, and reject God out of hand. But other people have an inkling that yes, God probably does exist. They're not sure what He/She/It is like, but having seen the incredible scale and diversity of our universe, not to mention the beautiful form and function of our own minds and bodies, together with our inbuilt (and sometimes very inconvenient) sense of right and wrong, it seems like a reasonable proposition.

The British astronomer Sir James Jeans certainly reached that conclusion. He wrote, "The universe appears to have been designed by a pure mathematician." For him, the breathtaking order of our universe – from the tiniest blood cell to the most distant galaxies – points to the existence of a master planner.

Tom Stoppard, one of the most celebrated and intellectually rigorous playwrights of our time, wrote a play called Jumpers. When asked to talk about the play's theme, Stoppard said:

> A straight line of evolution from amino acid all the way through to Shakespeare's sonnets – that strikes me as possible, but a very long shot. Why back such an outsider? However preposterous the idea of God is, it seems to have an edge of plausibility.

"Atheism is a crutch for those who can't accept the reality of God", one of his characters says.

One other factor that has led some people to feel that God might exist is the human sense of loneliness, emptiness and restlessness, not to mention our sense of the infinite. That's why the background story of The Matrix is so ingenious: it feels like it might be true. In the film, Morpheus tells Neo:

> Let me tell you why you are here. It's because you know
> something. What you know you can't explain, but you
> feel it. You've felt it your entire life. There is something
> wrong with the world. You don't know what it is, but it's
> there, like a splinter in your mind, driving you mad.

And it often seems as if nothing we do stops us feeling
that way. A great job isn't enough. The car we've always
wanted isn't enough. Friends aren't enough. Marriage
and money aren't enough. Thom Yorke of the band
Radiohead, in an interview with the New Musical
Express, was asked about his ambitions:

> Ambitious for what? What for? I thought when I got to
> where I wanted to be everything would be different.
> I'd be somewhere else. I thought it'd be all white fluffy
> clouds. And then I got there. And I'm still here.

The interviewer asked him why he carried on making
music, even though he'd already achieved the critical
and commercial success he hoped for. "It's filling the
hole. That's all anyone does." To the question, "What
happens to the hole?", Yorke paused a long time before
answering: "It's still there."

What Morpheus and Thom Yorke describe is nothing
new. Augustine, writing in the fifth century, suggested
a reason for this sense of "wrongness" in our lives: "O
God, you have made us for yourself, and our hearts are
restless till they find their rest in you." Could he be right?

Having a vague sense that God might exist is one thing.
According to recent polls, between 70 and 80 per cent
of people in the UK have just that vague sense. But to
believe that God actually cares intimately for those he

has created probably seems a bit far-fetched to many. However, that is the claim the Bible makes. Furthermore, the Bible says, we can know God personally.

Imagine that you wanted to get to know the Queen personally. You could try writing a letter, or perhaps ringing Buckingham Palace, or you could try standing outside the palace gates with a very big sign. I don't recommend flying a light aircraft into her garden, because the last person who tried that – funnily enough, an author trying to get some free publicity for his book – got arrested.

The fact is, you wouldn't get very far with any of these approaches. Your only chance would be if she decided she wanted to meet you, and introduced herself personally. And that is exactly what the Bible says God has done in Jesus Christ. That's the beginning of the good news Mark has for us. It tells us that God wants to meet us, in person, and the life and death of Jesus Christ is the way he's chosen to do it.

Our choice

Now, if the Bible's claim is true – that our creator wants to meet us through Jesus Christ – then that would affect all of us, whether we like it or not. Of course, we could choose to avoid investigating this claim. Alternatively, we could choose to examine the claim to see if it is true. But I am duty-bound to say that each of these choices will have serious implications for us.

A few years ago, a London newspaper conducted a revealing experiment. They had a person stand outside Oxford Circus underground station and offer people leaflets. On each was written a simple instruction: Bring this piece of paper back to the person who gave it to you and they will give you £5. People swarmed by, and lots actually took the leaflet, but in three hours only eleven came back. Apparently, most of us automatically assume that these bits of paper will be of no real interest, that they won't do us any good. So we either don't bother to read them, or we refuse to believe them.

My only plea is that you don't make that assumption. Don't assume that you've heard it all before, and that reading the Bible will be of no use to you. Instead, I ask you simply to give it the benefit of the doubt as we focus on one book of the Bible, a book named after its author, Mark. It's an accurate account of one life, Jesus' life, written with the insight of a man who spent years by Jesus' side.[1] (For more on why we can trust the Bible, see the chapter in *If you could ask God one question* by Paul Williams and Barry Cooper.)

By making time to read Mark, you may begin to see – as I did – that Jesus Christ is the most conclusive proof anyone could have, not only that God exists, but also that he made you and that he cares passionately for you. In fact, Jesus answers all the difficult questions we posed a few paragraphs ago.

And if those kinds of answers frighten you, then, as they say before the football scores on the news, "look away now…"

---

1 Mark was guided as he wrote by an actual eyewitness of the events he describes. The evidence suggests that the eyewitness was a man called Peter, a close friend of Jesus. As we're about to see, Peter plays a key role in the events that are about to unfold.

2.
A QUESTION OF IDENTITY

A few years ago I was invited out to lunch, and as I'd arrived a bit early, I waited on the stairs just off the main dining room. Standing opposite me on the stairs was another diner. I vaguely recognised him, but thought nothing of it, so – as English people do – we gave each other a sheepish nod, and then stood there awkwardly in total silence for 5 whole minutes, from 12.55 until 1 o'clock.

At 1 o'clock, a man emerged from around the corner, looked up at the man beside me and exclaimed, "Ah, William, there you are, we're in the private dining room."

Turns out it was Prince William.

I'd been standing with him all that time, he had nothing better to do than talk to me, and I hadn't said a single word. Sadly, all I saw was a handsome, well-dressed 25 year-old with thinning blond hair. What I didn't see was my future King. Because I didn't get his identity right, I related to him in completely the wrong way.

Now in this case, it didn't really matter. Yes, I missed out on a once-in-a-lifetime conversation (and arguably so did he), but that's about it.

Sometimes, though, it really does matter. Because if we don't get Jesus' identity right, we'll relate to him in totally the wrong way, and we may end up ignoring him completely. And missing this King's identity would be disastrous.

That's why Mark gives us the historical evidence we need so that we can recognise Jesus for who he is. Was he a great moral teacher? A compassionate miracle-worker? A misunderstood revolutionary? Mark's verdict goes far beyond any of these, as you can see from the very first sentence in his book:

> The beginning of the gospel about Jesus Christ...

The playwright Noel Coward was once asked, "What do you think about God?", to which he replied, "We've never been properly introduced." Well, that's exactly what Mark wants to do for us here. "Christ" isn't Jesus' second name. It's a title, like President or Prime Minister. And it means "God's only chosen King", a unique person with divine authority. God in human form.

Now, to say such a thing seems outrageous to many modern ears, but it was no small matter to the people of Mark's day either. In fact, it got you thrown to the lions, because the only person you were supposed to treat with that kind of reverence was the Roman Emperor.

Virgil, the Roman poet, described the emperors as a "new breed of Man, come down from Heaven". But here, right at the start of his book, Mark boldly tells us that no, there is a higher authority than the Emperor, and his name is Jesus. Mark then tries to justify this outrageous claim by providing evidence from Jesus' life.

Jesus has power and authority to teach

One piece of evidence Mark gives concerning Jesus' identity is in chapter 1 verses 21 and 22:

> They [Jesus and some followers] went to Capernaum, and when the Sabbath came, Jesus went into the synagogue and began to teach. The people were amazed at his teaching, because he taught them as one who had authority, not as the teachers of the law.

One of the things that set Jesus apart from the religious leaders of the day (the "teachers of the law") was the way he taught. The teachers of the law didn't come up with their own material. As with most of my sermons, the best stuff was borrowed from other people. There was nothing original in their teaching. They never taught without quoting the great teachers of the past, and they never claimed any authority of their own.

But Jesus did not teach like that. He didn't hide behind anybody else's authority – he claimed authority of his own. Rather than use the great teachers of the past to back up his arguments, he talks about himself. He says, "I'm telling you this on my own authority – you can take it from me." It's like someone in court who, rather than swearing on the Bible, simply says, "I give you my word; there is no higher guarantee of truth".

Jesus not only claims that his words have as much authority as God's words: when he speaks, it's as if somebody has suddenly switched on the lights in a dark room. His hearers are not merely impressed by his teaching, they are "amazed". What people in the synagogue heard from the lips of Jesus explained their lives to them. His teaching provided clear answers to the most difficult, obscure questions. And all this from a man who had no education to speak of.

We would, however, have every right to be even more wary of someone who claimed his teaching had the same authority as God's, if his own life didn't match up to that teaching. At the age of 16, I started keeping a diary because I felt I owed it to the world to enshrine for posterity quite how great a bloke I was. What I found as I wrote in the diary was the contradiction between what I said about myself and what I actually did. I was surprisingly selfish, despite some good intentions, and I often ignored my words and ideals when it came to getting what I wanted.

But Jesus was no hypocrite. His life was totally consistent with his teaching. He teaches, for example: "Love your enemies and pray for those who persecute you."[2] Later on, as he is suffering the most cruel and painful death imaginable, he prays, "Father, forgive them, for they do not know what they are doing."[3] Now that is practising what you preach.

So that's Mark's first point: Jesus has power and authority to teach.

Jesus has power and authority over sickness
But Jesus was no mere teacher. Another piece of evidence Mark provides about Jesus' identity concerns his power and authority over sickness. One example of this is found in chapter 1 verses 29 to 31:

---

2 Matthew 5:44
3 Luke 23:34

> As soon as they left the synagogue, they went with James and John to the home of Simon and Andrew. Simon's mother-in-law was in bed with a fever, and they told Jesus about her. So he went to her, took her hand and helped her up. The fever left her and she began to wait on them.

This is not an isolated incident. Three verses later, in verse 34, we read that Jesus cures whole crowds of sick people. A few days later, his touch cures a man who was suffering with a disease so serious that most people would have avoided any contact with the victim at all. But Jesus does reach out to touch him, and his simple touch is enough to cure his leprosy completely and immediately.

In fact, Jesus' power over sickness is such that even a word from his lips is enough to cure the most hopeless of cases. In the second chapter of Mark, for example, we read about a paralytic man who had to be lowered through a roof to meet Jesus – such was the density of the crowd that pressed to see him.

He says to the paralytic, "Get up, take your mat and go home" and, in full view of everyone, the man gets up and walks out, taking his mat with him. Not surprisingly, later in the chapter, everyone is saying, "We have never seen anything like this!" The deaf hear, the blind see and the lame walk.

Mark records 12 such examples of Jesus healing, and all of them show that Jesus' authority over sickness is far, far greater than that of modern doctors – despite 2000 years' worth of advances in science and medicine.

Neither did these striking events go unnoticed by non-Christians of the time. For example, Josephus, a Jewish historian writing in Section 18 of his book Antiquities, called Jesus "a doer of wonderful deeds". It's hard to disagree with that diagnosis.

Jesus has power and authority over nature

Mark shows that Jesus is an extraordinary teacher and healer, but in chapter 4 he goes even further.

> Jesus and his followers (usually called "disciples" in the Bible) are in a boat on the Lake of Galilee when a "furious squall" comes up. Indeed, the original Greek word translated "furious squall" is actually closer to our word "whirlwind". It is a whirlwind so intense that waves break over their boat, which practically sinks.

And the disciples – some of whom are hardened fishermen – are convinced they are going to die. In their panic they wake Jesus, who is in the stern "sleeping on a cushion": "Teacher, don't you care if we drown?"

What Jesus does next is staggering.

> He got up, rebuked the wind and said to the waves, "Quiet! Be still!" Then the wind died down and it was completely calm.

It can take waves days to die down, but Jesus flattens them with a few words. At this stage, you could be forgiven for thinking, "But that's impossible – human beings can't do that kind of thing." And I'd agree with you. But that's exactly Mark's point: Jesus was not just another human being. Normal rules no longer apply. To be honest, I couldn't still my bathwater with a word, let alone a furious storm.

But that is exactly what this great teacher and healer

does. And, in the light of this incident, is it enough to call Jesus "a great teacher and healer"? For Mark, and for the startled disciples on that boat, it is not. They know that only God himself has control over the elements. So, looking at each other in terror, the disciples ask, "Who is this? Even the wind and the waves obey him!" Whatever conclusion they – and we – draw, one thing is clear: Jesus has power and authority over nature.

But in the next chapter, these disciples witness something even more amazing. They see Jesus exert the same degree of control over death itself.

Jesus has power and authority over death

The author Susan Cheever wrote, "Death is terrifying because it is so ordinary. It happens all the time." Philip Larkin, whose poems often concerned death, lived most of his life tormented by the thought of it. For him, even life itself was "slow dying".

But for some, especially the young, death seems a long way off. Another poet, Siegfried Sassoon, who lost many loved ones in World War I, wrote that "at the age of twenty-two, I believed myself to be inextinguishable".

There are many others who share that youthful bravado. I was certainly like that until the age of 16, when my godfather died after having lost his footing on a cliff path. Before that happened, I had no idea of the pain involved in death. And I'm not just talking about the pain felt by the person who is dying.

There's the pain and despair felt by the family, the friends, all of whom feel the terrible sense of being separated from someone forever. Someone who loved and understood them. And those kinds of relationships are so hard to come by.

I remember picking up a bereavement card in a hospital shop, and on the inside it read: "Those whom we have loved never really go away." But that's a lie. That's the whole problem. The reason death is so fearful is because it has absolute power to separate us totally from those we love, often unexpectedly. And there's no comeback, no opportunity to tell them we love them one last time. There's nothing we can do to save them from it, however hard we wish. But, in the passage we'll look at now, Jesus confronts death as its master. Although we are powerless in the face of death, Jesus displays total authority over it.

In chapter 5 of Mark, there is a religious leader called Jairus. His little daughter is dying. And agonizingly, he is powerless to do anything about it. He falls at Jesus' feet and pleads with him to help, which is no small thing for a respected ruler at the local synagogue. He is desperate.

So Jesus agrees to go with him to his house. As they are making their way there, something terrible happens.

> ...some men came from the house of Jairus, the synagogue ruler. "Your daughter is dead," they said. "Why bother the teacher any more?"

And, in that instant, the man's fragile hopes are shattered. They're too late. She's gone forever.

But then we read:

> Ignoring what they said, Jesus told the synagogue ruler, "Don't be afraid; just believe."

It's a brave man who says something like that to a distraught father. A brave man – or at least one who is supremely confident of his own power.

> He did not let anyone follow him except Peter, James and John the brother of James. When they came to the home of the synagogue ruler, Jesus saw a commotion, with people crying and wailing loudly. He went in and said to them, "Why all this commotion and wailing? The child is not dead but asleep." But they laughed at him.
> After he put them all out, he took the child's father and mother and the disciples who were with him, and went in where the child was. He took her by the hand and said to her, "Talitha koum!" (which means, "Little girl, I say to you, get up!"). Immediately the girl stood up and walked around (she was twelve years old). At this they were completely astonished.

You can't get much more shocking than that. The man hears the terrible words, "Your daughter is dead", but Jesus tells him not to worry, just to trust in his power over death. The child isn't dead, Jesus insists, she is merely sleeping. Thinking that he is speaking literally, the mourners laugh at him. They've seen the corpse. But Jesus takes the corpse's hand, tells her to get up, and she does so. The point is clear: for Jesus, it is as easy to raise somebody from the dead as it is for us to rouse somebody from sleep.

The challenge to us is this: having seen Jesus' authority over death, do we trust him enough to trust him with our own death?

I remember being with a dying woman in a cancer

hospice. Because she, like Jairus, had placed her trust in Jesus, I was able to say to her with confidence: "You are going to sleep and Christ will wake you from that sleep." But this awakening will not be reincarnation, or a temporary release from death, like the one Jairus' daughter experienced. This will be resurrection: unending life, in a new body that is specially designed to enjoy a stunning new creation. A creation no longer blighted by suffering, disease or death.

If we need more proof that Jesus can do this for us, we need look no further than Jesus' own death, and subsequent resurrection. We'll look at both in chapters 4 and 5, but can I say at this point that, if Jesus does have power over death, then it is madness to ignore him, to say "I'm just not interested" or "I don't have time" or "That's nice, but it's not for me." One day you and I will die. We may not fear it yet, but we can be absolutely certain of it. So Jesus' apparent power to overcome death is definitely worthy of our investigation.

But believe it or not, "Quiet! Be still!" and "Get up!" are not the most outrageous things Jesus says. For that, we're going to return to chapter 2 of Mark's Gospel, to the story of a paralytic man lowered through the roof by his friends.

Jesus has power and authority to forgive sins

> Some men came, bringing to him a paralytic, carried by four of them. Since they could not get him to Jesus because of the crowd, they made an opening in the roof above Jesus and, after digging through it, lowered the mat the paralysed man was lying on. (Mark 2:3-4)

I can't imagine what the owner of the house thought as he saw his roof torn open. Or what Jesus thought as his words were interrupted by dust and sunlight pouring from the ceiling.

I've had public talks interrupted in creative ways. I can remember one talk during which a person punched someone else in the face, and another in which someone decided to set fire to my clipboard. But I can't ever remember anyone actually dismantling the roof above my head, and then lowering someone through it.

However, what is most striking here is the first thing Jesus says to the paralysed man:

> When Jesus saw their faith, he said to the paralytic, "Son, your sins are forgiven."

To the untrained eye, the man's most obvious problem would appear to be his inability to walk – so why not deal with that first? Why does Jesus home in on the problem of the man's "sins"?

"Sin" is an old-fashioned word to many people. It has lost its meaning. When The Independent newspaper ran an article on the seven deadly sins, the writer had this to say: "In this day and age, sin has lost its sting. A bit of sinning is much more likely to be seen as a spot of grown-up naughtiness; the kind of thing that sends a delicious shock through the system." That's how most people think of sin – as a bit of fun on the side.

However, rightly understood, there is nothing nice about it. Jesus repeatedly insists that sin is our biggest problem – not paralysis, not global warming, not terrorism, not unemployment, not lack of love or education, but sin.

According to the Bible, sin is ignoring God in the world he has made.

But why is ignoring God in this way so serious? Because it cuts us off from God. Because every time I insist on my independence in a world where God sustains everything, I am cutting myself off from the very source of all life. The Bible is clear that to live like that results in death – and not just death here, but eternal death.

As he talks to the paralysed man, Jesus makes the staggering claim that he has the authority to forgive this "sin" which cuts us off from God: "Son, your sins are forgiven." The implications of this statement are not lost on the religious teachers who are sitting nearby. They don't mind the paralytic being called a sinner; they know from their Scriptures that everyone is a sinner. No, their problem with what Jesus says is more straightforward: "He's blaspheming! Who can forgive sins but God alone?"

They know that if we sin against God, only God can forgive us. (After all, if I wrong a person, only that person has the right to forgive me; it's nobody else's business.) By claiming to have forgiven the sins of the paralytic man, Jesus is putting himself in God's place. The religious teachers are deeply offended by this. But, as if to back up his claim, Jesus immediately heals the man with a few words.

Jesus not only talks as if he is God, he also acts with God's power. So, once again, the question confronts us: just who is this man?

Mark's answer is clear. Jesus is the Christ, "the Lord" over sickness, nature, death and sin. Here, as he teaches, calms the storm, raises the dead, heals the sick and forgives sin, he is acting in God's world with God's authority. He behaves as if he is ruler over everything, as if he is God himself.

And if that is true – that Jesus is God – then things start getting very personal for us as readers of Mark. Will I allow Jesus to be my Lord and teacher? Do I recognize that he has authority over my death, whether I like it or not? Can I see that he has the authority to forgive my sin, or to leave it unforgiven?

3.
BENEATH THE SURFACE

When I was a student, I joined the local rugby club. Now the club was very competitive, so during the summer I received a long and strenuous training schedule in preparation for what was called "Club Pre-Season Testing and Training" in September. I dutifully circled the date on my calendar, before throwing the schedule away and thinking, "I'll go on some runs and do some sit-ups – I'll be fine."

September rolled around eventually, after a fairly casual summer in which I nevertheless did more exercise than I had ever done before. In fact, I felt pretty confident as I turned up at the training ground. As I walked into the changing room, however, I noticed that all the blokes were very quiet. You spot this very quickly if it occurs in rugby players. Then the coach came in and said, "Right, we'll start with the bleep test."

For the bleep test, we ran back and forth over a 20-yard stretch in time to a bleep that got faster and faster. We literally ran until we dropped. In my case, the "drop" part was not long in coming. I was the second to drop out, having collapsed and been physically sick.

Immediately after that, it was time for the fat tests. We had to strip down to our shorts, which, as people who know me would tell you, is a terrifying thought. A machine with a large set of tweezers pinched the flesh on our biceps, triceps, stomachs, sides, thighs and calves. (There was one bloke who had an even higher percentage of body fat than I did. We became firm friends.)

And so the tests went on. The results of each were recorded, and each test was – to a greater or lesser degree – humiliating. When it was finally over, the coach said, "Well, it's not comfortable, but at least we've found out the truth here on the training ground before the real questions get asked out there on the playing field. Some of you have really been exposed, haven't you?"

Listening to what Jesus has to say about you and me is like going through fitness tests. It means being told what we are really like beneath the surface, and it is a very uncomfortable experience. In a way, a better title for this chapter would be "I wish I didn't have to tell you this, but…"

The last chapter described Jesus' unique power and authority to teach, cure illness, calm storms and raise the dead. He spoke and acted as if he were God come to earth. But why come at all? What was Jesus' aim, according to Mark's Gospel? Did he want to bring peace on earth? Did he want to end the sufferings of the world? Did he want to give us a supreme example of how we should live and treat each other? Or was he aiming to bring about the reform of society? Although there is an element of truth in all of those possibilities, Mark's Gospel doesn't give any of them as Jesus' ultimate aim.

Jesus came to rescue rebels

Mark wants us to know that the reason Jesus came was to rescue "sinners": those who have rebelled against God. Look at chapter 2 verses 15 to 17:

> While Jesus was having dinner at Levi's house, many tax collectors and "sinners" were eating with him and his disciples, for there were many who followed him. When the teachers of the law who were Pharisees saw him eating with the "sinners" and tax collectors, they asked his disciples: "Why does he eat with tax collectors and 'sinners'?"
> On hearing this, Jesus said to them, "It is not the healthy who need a doctor, but the sick. I have not come to call the righteous, but sinners."

In this passage there are two groups of people: the goodies and the baddies. (Stop me if I'm getting too technical.) The baddies are made up of people such as Levi, who is a tax collector. Bear in mind that tax collectors were even less popular then than they are now. In fact, they were reviled as traitors, working as they did for the occupying Roman forces.

The goodies in this passage are the senior religious figures of the day, the Pharisees. They are the religious establishment, their credentials as religious people are hugely impressive, and they are known as being the most religious people around.

The question is: who would you expect Jesus to associate with? The tax collector, or the local church leader? Instinctively we'd expect him to want to be with the goodies, the religious people, the elite. It would be a bit like a school prize-giving, with Jesus patting the religious do-gooders on the back, while scum like Levi enviously look on.

But this is the shock for us (as it was for them): "It is not the healthy who need a doctor, but the sick. I have not come to call the righteous, but sinners."

It upsets the religious people enormously to hear this powerful and authoritative figure say, "I can heal you, but if you don't think you need a cure, you can forget it. I'm here for the sick." Jesus makes it clear that people who think they are good enough without him don't want his help, just as healthy people don't want doctors. That's a problem for a lot of us. As Tom Ripley says in *The Talented Mr Ripley*: "Whatever you do, however terrible, however hurtful, it all makes sense, doesn't it, in your head? You never meet anybody that thinks they're a bad person."

But Jesus says here, "I've come for people who realize that they're bad people, for those who know that they're living as rebels in God's world." In other words, for sinners.

So the qualification for coming to Jesus is not "Are you good enough?", but "Are you bad enough?" I can't tell you what a shock this was to me when I saw it for the first time. My idea of Jesus as I grew up was that he was only interested in good people. I had no idea that he came to call sinners.

Jesus' aim, then, is to call rebels back into a relationship with the God who made them, with the God who gives them each breath and yet is treated like a footnote in their lives.

In the next chapter we'll see exactly how Jesus achieves that rescue, but for now I want to focus on the assumption Jesus makes: that we are all rebels in need of rescue, even if we believe we're basically good people.

We are all rebels

There is a certain irony when Jesus refers to the Pharisees as "righteous" ("I have not come to call the righteous, but sinners"). Jesus recognizes that, although the Pharisees are righteous by their own standards, they are not righteous by God's standards. If we are in any doubt about this, fast forward to Mark chapter 3 where these Pharisees, these people who consider themselves good enough for God, begin jealously plotting to kill Jesus. Clearly, despite what they may think, the Pharisees need rescuing just as much as anyone else does. Jesus makes it quite clear that everyone – however "good" they consider themselves to be – is in desperate need of rescue.

If that idea grates with you, as it certainly once did with me, then we need to expose ourselves to a tough question: what is the world really like?

If we take an honest look at the world, we will see good and evil mixed together. We take a stroll in the park and see a little child toddle excitedly towards its mother with arms outstretched. Nearby is a young couple ambling slowly along, lost in each other's company. When we see those kinds of things we think – quite rightly – that this world is a pretty special place. Louis Armstrong sang it beautifully:

I see skies of blue, and clouds of white,
The bright blessed day, the dark sacred night,
And I think to myself, what a wonderful world.

But it can all change in an instant. If the child in the park falls over and starts screaming, we remember that pain is never far behind happiness. If the loving couple starts shouting angrily at one another, we remember the newspaper article revealing that half of all marriages end in divorce. The world is certainly not all bad, but who can honestly claim that it's all good?

At least one hundred million people died violent deaths during the one hundred years of the twentieth century. That's more than during the previous 19 centuries put together. It seems safe to say that war and death are as much a part of our world as peace and life.

Yes, Louis Armstrong was right to say that it's a wonderful world, but we have to admit that there is something profoundly wrong with it, too. We sense that the world could be, should be, a wonderful place – but the reality repeatedly dashes our hopes.

The Bible says that we have our sense of what should be because God made you and me "in his image". In other words, because we are like him in lots of ways, we also have his sense of perfection. The Bible goes on to say that the reason the world is not the way it should be is because we are not the way we should be. That, says Jesus, is why we need rescuing.

And yet it still offends us to think that we need anyone's help. Of course, some people are definitely "bad" – murderers, rapists and paedophiles for a start – but not us, and certainly not our family and our friends.

We're basically good people with a few human faults here and there.

We tend to be confident that our good points outweigh the bad, that we are good enough for God. But at this point we need to ask another tough question: what are we really like? The truth is that we're much more flawed than we're often willing to admit.

I came across this gleeful advertisement recently on the internet:

> **You're in Serious Trouble – It's a Proven Fact!**
> Deleting "Internet Cache and History" will NOT protect you, because any of the web pages, pictures, movies, videos, sounds, e-mail, chat logs and everything else you see or do could easily be recovered to haunt you forever! How would you feel if a snoop made this information public to your spouse, mother and father, neighbours, children, boss or the media? It could easily ruin your life!

The people who wrote that certainly understood that human beings are susceptible to great weakness. I understood this fact for myself when my brother once challenged me to think, say and do nothing impure, unkind or untrue for 15 minutes (I don't think I made it past the first minute).

And it's not only the things we've said, done and thought that are a problem. There are the things we didn't say, do and think. People we should have helped, perhaps. Those lapses which may have bothered our consciences at the time but which were forgotten an hour or two later. Or there may be other, more bitter failures that we have never been able to forget. If all my thoughts, words and actions were displayed for all my friends and family to see, it would be a nightmare. I wouldn't even be able to make eye contact with them, I would be so ashamed.

So what's the problem? Why is there so much to be ashamed of? Verses 18 to 23 of Mark chapter 7 have the answer. The Pharisees have been arguing that it's the external things that make us "bad": the things we touch, the places we go, the things we eat. But Jesus tells his disciples that the problem is much closer to home:

> "Are you so dull?" he asked. "Don't you see that nothing that enters a man from the outside can make him 'unclean'? For it doesn't go into his heart but into his stomach, and then out of his body."... He went on: "What comes out of a man is what makes him 'unclean'. For from within, out of men's hearts, come evil thoughts, sexual immorality, theft, murder, adultery, greed, malice, deceit, lewdness, envy, slander, arrogance and folly. All these evils come from inside and make a man 'unclean'."[4]

The problem, says Jesus, is our hearts. They make us "unclean". If we were to trace all the evil in the world back to its source, says Jesus, the place we'd end up is the human heart.

To the people of Jesus' day, the heart wasn't just the pump that sent blood around the body. It wasn't simply the emotional core of a human being. It was even more than that: it was "the real you", the inner you, the seat of human personality. Why is it so hard to keep good

---

4 For the sake of clarity, I should point out that the word "man" here refers to all mankind (in other words, all human beings).

relationships going? Why do we hurt even those we love most? Why aren't people at work more co-operative? Because each of us has a heart problem.

Unfortunately, according to Jesus, our problems don't end there. It's not just the fact that we often treat each other in a shameful way: we treat God in that way too. (And just as there are consequences when we treat other human beings carelessly, so there are consequences when we treat God in that way too.) Look at Mark chapter 12 verses 28 to 31, where Jesus is debating with some religious leaders:

> One of the teachers of the law came and heard them debating. Noticing that Jesus had given them a good answer, he asked him, "Of all the commandments, which is the most important?"

This was a famously tricky question to answer. Which of God's commands is the most important? All the religious leaders debated it endlessly. After all, God made us and sustains us. He gives us every good thing we enjoy. Not only that, he has power and authority over our lives. So how should we respond to him? Jesus tells us:

> Love the Lord your God with all your heart and with all your soul and with all your mind and with all your strength.

Note the word "all". No part of our life is to be cordoned off from God. The appropriate response to a God who made us, gives us every breath, and is deeply and personally committed to us is that we should love him with all we are and all we have. But is that the way things are?

Back in the day, Whitney Houston used to sing "learning to love yourself is the greatest love of all". But the tragic fact is that by doing so, we turn our backs on the greatest love for which we were primarily designed. You and I were designed first and foremost to love God.

Rather than loving God with all our hearts, as Jesus commands, we live as if we were God, ignoring the one who gives us all that we cherish: love, friends, laughter – even life itself. We decide what is right and wrong, we are our only point of reference, and we are the highest authority. We ignore the very person who is keeping us alive.

We are in danger

The passengers on the doomed ocean liner Titanic didn't know that they were heading for trouble. As they headed for the iceberg, they were having the party of their lives. All they felt on deck were three small shudders as the ice gouged a hole below the waterline. Presumably, given that everything seemed fine, there were even those who deliberately ignored the warnings to get to safety.

But whether they liked it or not, the reality was that every single person on that ship was in serious danger.

Let's look now at the hardest-hitting verses of Mark's Gospel in order to determine the reality of our own situation. In these verses – Mark chapter 9 verses 43 to 48 – Jesus himself warns us just how serious our sin really is:

> "If your hand causes you to sin, cut it off. It is better
> for you to enter life maimed than with two hands to go
> into hell, where the fire never goes out. And if your foot

causes you to sin, cut it off. It is better for you to enter life crippled than to have two feet and be thrown into hell. And if your eye causes you to sin, pluck it out. It is better for you to enter the kingdom of God with one eye than to have two eyes and be thrown into hell, where "their worm does not die, and the fire is not quenched".

Because of our sin, we are in terrible danger of facing God's judgment. And when we stop for a moment to think about it, the fact that sin matters to God is a very good thing. It means that how I treat you matters to God, and how you treat me matters to him too.

In the verses above, Jesus speaks of hell as a place where, for all eternity, people will be punished if they die still rebelling against their Creator. It will be a real place of conscious pain. Believe me, I take no pleasure in relating these words of Christ, just as God takes no pleasure in punishing people. The reason Jesus warns us about hell is because he loves us and does not want us to go there.

When I was in Australia staying with a friend, he took me to a beach on Botany Bay. It was deserted, the sun was out, and the clear water was completely calm. I decided I had to go for a swim, but just as I was taking off my shirt, my friend said in a broad Aussie accent,

"Mate, what are you doing?"

I told him I was going for a dip.

"But what about those signs?", he said, pointing to a huge billboard behind me.

It read: "Danger – Sharks. No Swimming." It seemed hard to believe, because everything looked so calm and beautiful.

I said, "Oh don't be ridiculous, I'll be fine."

To which my Aussie friend said, very dryly, "Listen, mate, 200 Australians have been killed by sharks over the years. You have to work out whether those signs are there to save you, or to ruin your fun. You're of age, you decide."

With that he walked off up the beach, and I rather sheepishly put my shirt back on.

The words of Jesus are like a huge warning sign to us. They have been written down in order to try and protect us. But many people – understandably – want to dismiss this disturbing idea of hell as a fairy tale. They don't see how serious their sin is. Like the passengers on the Titanic, they are blind to the fact that they need to be rescued.

But ask yourself this question: if hell is not a reality, why did Jesus bother coming at all? "I have not come to call the righteous, but sinners." If sinners don't really need rescuing, why the rescue mission?

According to Jesus, hell is real. So much so that we should do anything to avoid it. "If your hand causes you to sin, cut it off. It is better for you to enter life maimed than with two hands to go into hell."

But here's the problem. Jesus is not giving us the cure for our sin when he talks about cutting off a hand or a foot, or gouging out an eye. Even if we were to do that, the knife would never go deep enough. Why? Because the problem is deep within us, in our hearts. And that is why we need Jesus to rescue us. "It is not the healthy who need a doctor, but the sick…"

As much as I hated the fat tests and the bleep tests, I

have to say that I would rather be exposed as unfit on the training ground than in front of spectators in a key match. That's exactly what Jesus does, exposing what we are really like so that we can do something about it while there is still time.

If there's no danger, we can forget about Jesus, put down this book, and get on with our lives. But if there is any possibility that we might face punishment from God for our rebellion, then ignoring Jesus would be as foolish as swimming with the sharks.

4.
THE DEATH THAT CHANGED EVERYTHING

I once picked up a biography of Winston Churchill and searched the index. Even though it was a fairly weighty book with about three hundred pages, only three pages were devoted to the subject of his death. In the Gospels (the books of Matthew, Mark, Luke and John in the Bible), about one third of each Gospel is given over to Jesus' death. We've seen how amazing his life was – so why spend so much time dwelling on his death?

Indeed, why is it that his mode of death – the cross – has become a universally-recognized symbol of Christianity? Christians might have chosen a manger to remind them of Jesus' birth, or an empty tomb to remind them of his resurrection. Perhaps a scroll to remind them of his teaching or a lamp to signify a brilliant life lived in an otherwise dark world. But no, they chose a cross – a reminder of his death. No other religion actively celebrates the death of its founder.

Not only that, but Christians celebrate the cross – a particularly horrendous Roman method of execution reserved for common criminals. The Roman orator Cicero described it like this:

> But the executioner, the veil that covers the condemned man's head, the cross of crucifixion, these are horrors which ought to be far removed not only from the person of a Roman citizen but even from his thoughts and his gaze and his hearing. It is utterly wrong that a Roman citizen, a free man, would ever be compelled to endure or tolerate such dreadful things.[5]

The cross was deliberately made cruel and gruesome so that any slave considering rebellion would pass by the crucified victim and think to himself, "However terrible my life is, rebellion is not worth it." Small wonder that the late comedian Bill Hicks observed: "A lot of Christians wear crosses around their necks. Do you think when Jesus comes back he's going to want to look at a cross?"

But Christians aren't ashamed of the cross. In fact, they seem proud of it. Paul, another writer in the Bible, says this: "May I never boast except in the cross of our Lord Jesus Christ".[6]

Why should this be? Take a look at Mark chapter 8 verse 31:

> He [Jesus] then began to teach them that the Son of Man [meaning himself] must suffer many things and be rejected by the elders, chief priests and teachers of the law, and that he must be killed and after three days rise again.

---

5 Cicero, *Murder Trials*, trans. Michael Grant (London: Penguin, 1990)
6 Galatians 6:14

Notice the word "must". Jesus is saying not only that he will die, but that his death is necessary in some way. Similarly, look at Jesus' words in Mark chapter 10 verse 45:

> For even the Son of Man did not come to be served, but to serve, and to give his life as a ransom for many.

The "Faith Zone" in London's Millennium Dome (remember that?) said that Jesus was a good man who died tragically young. But that misses the point. Jesus died in order to pay "a ransom for many". He died to rescue rebels by paying the price to free them from sin. Suddenly, the thought of celebrating the cross seems less strange. Because although the danger we are in is very real, the cross is our lifeboat. It is how Jesus rescues people.

And to understand this fully, we need to read Mark's account of the crucifixion in chapter 15, which tells us three things about the cross: God was angry, Jesus was abandoned and we can be accepted.

God was angry

To God-fearing Jews of the time, darkness in the daytime was a sign of God's anger. Often in the Bible, light represents God's presence and favour, while darkness tells us that God is acting in judgment. For example, God judged Pharaoh by sending darkness over the land when he refused to release the Jews from slavery in Egypt.

Now, in Mark chapter 15 verse 33, we read about this startling incident that occurs while Jesus is on the cross:

> At the sixth hour [12 noon] darkness came over the whole land until the ninth hour [3 p.m.].

Mark counts the hours according to the Jewish system of timekeeping, and he tells us that, just when the sun should be burning brightest, at midday, darkness suddenly falls. A bit like a solar eclipse, except that this couldn't have been a solar eclipse. The crucifixion happened during the Jewish festival of Passover, which always fell on a full moon – but the moon cannot be full if it is positioned between the sun and the earth for an eclipse.

It's also worth remembering that solar eclipses never last more than six minutes. This darkness lasted three hours.

Mark wants us to understand that something supernatural is occurring, and the clear message is that God is angry.

Sometimes people think of anger as something irrational, unpredictable and wild. Some of us have seen that kind of anger in ourselves, in friends and close relatives, and we know how ugly it is. But God's anger is different. It is his controlled, personal hostility towards all that is wrong.

And if you think about it, a God who is good is right to be angry about wrong. Lying, selfishness, greed, exploitation, adultery, murder: assuming we care about other people at all, those things will make us angry. We cry out for justice. So is it unreasonable to expect that they will also anger the perfectly just God who made us?

All wrongdoing – all sin – matters to God, and the most serious wrongdoing of all occurs when the creatures he has lovingly created use their God-given freedom to rebel against him.

So, as Jesus was dying on the cross, the darkness that

came over the whole land tells us that God was justly acting in anger to punish sin.

Jesus was abandoned

There is no doubt that Jesus suffered great physical agony on the cross, but the information Mark relays here in chapter 15 verse 34 speaks of spiritual agony:

> And at the ninth hour Jesus cried out in a loud voice,
> "Eloi, Eloi, lama sabachthani?" – which means, "My God,
> my God, why have you forsaken me?"

On the cross, God the Son was "forsaken" by God the Father. Jesus experienced what it meant to be abandoned by his loving Father for the first time in all eternity.

Previously, Jesus had addressed God as "Father", or "Abba", a word even more warm and intimate than "Daddy". But not here. Here, it is simply "My God". Jesus is experiencing an unimaginably horrific and terrible separation, the like of which he has never known before. God the Father is doing something he only ever does by way of punishment.

But God the Son had never rebelled against God the Father. According to those who knew him, Jesus lived a perfectly sinless life. He had done nothing that deserved punishment. So why was he being punished? The answer is that he was taking the punishment for our sin.

Imagine a video that captures every detail of your life. In fact, it reveals far more than can be captured by any number of closed-circuit TV cameras: this video records your thoughts and your motives, as well as your actions and words. It's a record that covers your entire life, from the very first cry in the delivery room, right the way through to the final gasp in the hospital ward.

As you watch the video, there are lots of moments to cherish and of which you can feel relatively proud. There are loving relationships, wonderful achievements, genuine honesty. You see plenty of things that are worthy of applause and approval, things that make you want to hit rewind so that you can watch them again and again.

But, of course, there are also many moments of which you rightly feel ashamed, moments that make you want to hit fast forward. Selfish actions, unkind thoughts, words you've only spoken because you knew you wouldn't be heard. And running through it all, like a director's commentary that you cannot switch off, the failure to love God with all our heart, soul, mind and strength.

All of it is recorded faithfully on the video. The question is: would we want it played in front of people we know?

Sir Arthur Conan Doyle, creator of Sherlock Holmes, sent a telegram as a joke one night to the twelve most respected people he could think of. It read: "Flee! All is revealed!"

Within 24 hours, six of those people had left the country in a panic. Like them, we all have secrets that we would hate to have exposed. The Bible's way of describing the video of our life is "the unfavourable record of our debts".[7] And this record of our debts (or "sin") separates us from God. In fact, the Bible says that God is so pure that even one frame from that video would be enough to separate us from him.

---

7 Colossians 2:14 (GNB)

When we ignore God, doing things "our way", treating him as if he's not really important at all, it's no cause for celebration. Because when we do that, it breaks our relationship with him. We have no cause to feel proud of those times when we've treated him as if he were a servant, then blamed him when things have not gone as we wanted them to. Can you imagine treating a friend like that? Would you expect that relationship to last long?

As we've seen, this treatment of God ultimately results in judgment. If we insist on living apart from him, he will give us what we insist upon. If we continue saying to him, "Leave me alone", there will come a day when God says, "I will". This is what the Bible calls hell: to be without God's blessings, forever. It means being without the love of others. It is to be utterly alone, with no hope and no comfort.

And that is why Jesus cried out, "My God, my God, why have you forsaken me?" as he hung on the cross. He was tasting the reality of that punishment for himself. And it couldn't have been his sin that made him feel separated from God, because the Bible tells us that Jesus was free from sin. No, it was our sin that separated him from God.

In those agonizing moments, Jesus was taking upon himself the punishment that our sin, everything on that video, deserves. The Bible tells us again and again that our rebellion against God deserves punishment, and punishment is exactly what Jesus endured on our behalf. As Jesus died on the cross, he willingly died for me, as my substitute, in my place, taking the punishment I deserve.

The result of this extraordinary self-sacrifice is simply this: Jesus paid the price for sin so that we never have to.

The stunning truth is that Jesus loved me enough to die for me – for me, and for every person who puts their trust in him.

We can be accepted

What Mark does in verses 37 and 38 seems strange. He records the moment of Jesus' death, but then turns his attention to something that happens simultaneously at the temple, on the other side of the city. He wants us to understand that the two events are connected in some way:

> With a loud cry, Jesus breathed his last.
> The curtain of the temple was torn in two from top to bottom.

As soon as Jesus dies, we're transported to the interior of Jerusalem's huge temple. We see an incredible thing. The temple curtain is 30 feet high and as thick as the span of a man's hand. It is made from a single piece of material. Suddenly we hear a thunderous ripping sound and the curtain falls to the ground in two pieces.

But we'll only understand why that matters when we realize what the curtain stood for.

On 11 November 1989, the Berlin Wall was broken down, showing that the Cold War between East and West had ended. In the same way, when the curtain in the temple was ripped in two, the Cold War between God and us was ended.

The curtain was actually a terrifying barrier to the "Holy of Holies", the heart of the temple where God was said to live. So holy was this place that only the High Priest could enter it once a year. Not just any person, and not even any priest, but only the High Priest, once he had performed an elaborate series of sacrifices and cleansing rituals, and then only once a year.

The whole system was designed to show that it is not an easy thing to come into the presence of God. This thick, towering curtain was like a huge "No Entry" sign. It very clearly said that it is impossible for sinful people like you and me to walk into God's presence.

Then suddenly, as Jesus dies, this curtain is ripped in two by God, from top to bottom. God is saying that the way is now open for us to enter his presence. The barriers are now down, and there is nothing to prevent us from enjoying a relationship with him. How is this made possible? Because Jesus was willing to be abandoned. He has taken God's anger on our behalf so that we can be accepted.

I once read a story about a man caught in a forest fire. He'd had a remarkable escape and was asked how he'd managed to survive. Apparently, as he saw the fire being swept toward him by the wind, he realized that the flames were moving too fast to run away from. Instead, he took a lighter from his pocket and started setting fire to the area immediately downwind of him.

Soon he had formed a patch of burned grass. He then stood in the middle of the burned patch and, although the fire overtook him, it could not burn the grass immediately around him because he had already burned it. The man knew that fire cannot burn the same patch of grass twice.

The story illustrates a biblical truth: when God's anger burned against the sin that Jesus took upon himself at the cross, it burned once and for all. Once the judgment falls, it cannot fall again. We can be accepted by God because the punishment we deserve has fallen – once and for all – on Jesus:

> He was despised and rejected by men,
> a man of sorrows, and familiar with suffering.
>   Like one from whom men hide their faces
> he was despised, and we esteemed him not.
>   Surely he took up our infirmities
> and carried our sorrows,
>   yet we considered him stricken by God,
> smitten by him, and afflicted.
>   But he was pierced for our transgressions,
> he was crushed for our iniquities;
> the punishment that brought us peace was upon him,
> and by his wounds we are healed.
>   We all, like sheep, have gone astray,
> each of us has turned to his own way;
> and the LORD has laid on him the iniquity of us all.[8]

It's a remarkable poem. Firstly, because it tells us that although "each of us has turned to his own way", God nevertheless wants to rescue us by sending someone who would pay the price for our wrongdoing. And second, because this description of what happened at the cross was written about seven hundred years before it actually happened. You can find the rest of the poem in Isaiah chapter 53.

---

8 Isaiah 53:4-6

So, how should we respond to the cross? Mark's account of the crucifixion in chapter 15 focuses not only on Jesus, but also on the reactions of those who witness the event. It is as if Mark is saying, "This is how others reacted to what happened at the cross. How will you react? What do you see as you look at the cross?"

Reaction One: The busy soldiers

When we first meet them, they are mocking Jesus – in particular his claim to be King of the Jews. The whole company spit on him and beat him, before leading him to the place of execution.

> They brought Jesus to the place called Golgotha (which means The Place of the Skull). Then they offered him wine mixed with myrrh, but he did not take it. And they crucified him.

There's a glimmer of compassion here because they know what Jesus is about to suffer. They offer him wine mixed with myrrh, a bitter drug to help dull the agony, but he will not take it. Then they crucify him. And what is their response to this agonizing spectacle?

> Dividing up his clothes, they cast lots to see what each would get.

For the soldiers, the greatest legacy of the cross will be the garments left by the dead man. They're absorbed in simply doing their job. And as they do so, they notice nothing special about him.

Here's a frightening thought: as they are "just doing their job", they miss the fact that this is the most important death in history. No doubt they are doing their job well, but in doing their duty they miss the real legacy of the cross – which is far more than a set of bloodstained clothes.

And there are millions of people today who are like these soldiers. They're occupied with work, with doing their duty, with paying the bills. The daily activities of their intense lives blind them to the true significance of the cross.

Reaction Two: The self-satisfied religious

The religious leaders are already convinced that they know the way to God, so Jesus Christ is irrelevant to them. And – as far as they're concerned – the cross proves it:

> ... the chief priests and the teachers of the law mocked him among themselves. "He saved others," they said, "but he can't save himself!"

They're convinced that they have their own means of gaining access to God, and it certainly doesn't involve anything as shameful and pathetic as the cross. Mark implies that religious people are often the most vicious opponents of the cross. Despite their "spiritual" appearance, they do not want to be accepted by God in this way. Because they think of themselves as good people, they believe they have absolutely no need of Jesus' rescue.

The cross is offensive to them, as it was to George Bernard Shaw, who stood up at a Christian meeting during which the cross was being explained and shouted,

"I will pay for my sin myself!" Again, such people are blind to the seriousness of sin, and therefore blind to the true significance of Jesus' death.

Reaction Three: The cowardly Pilate

Pontius Pilate is the Roman governor of the area. The sign he has had put up over Jesus' head appears sympathetic. It reads: "The King of the Jews". All the Gospel writers assure us that Pilate is convinced of Jesus' innocence. He tries again and again to free Jesus from the clutches of the religious authorities who are exerting tremendous pressure on Pilate to have Jesus killed.

But, eventually, he hands Jesus over to be crucified. He knows deep down in his heart that Jesus doesn't deserve to be crucified, and so he utters those chilling words recorded by Matthew, another Gospel writer: "I am innocent of this man's blood. It's your responsibility!"

Why, then, does he hand over an innocent man to be executed? The answer lies in Mark chapter 15 verse 15:

> Wanting to satisfy the crowd, Pilate released Barabbas to them. He had Jesus flogged, and handed him over to be crucified.

Pilate is a crowd-pleaser. Like many people, he is unwilling to stand out from the crowd, and he buckles under pressure from those around him. His nerve cracks and he gives in to the desires of others, even though he knows Jesus is innocent. When it really matters, when the world is against him, he won't stand up for Jesus.

Pilate was a coward who abandoned an innocent man. And although he was blind to it at the time, Pilate abandoned someone who was a great deal more than that.

Reaction Four: The bystander who came for the show
Mark then records the reaction of an individual in the crowd:

> One man ran, filled a sponge with wine vinegar, put it on
> a stick, and offered it to Jesus to drink. "Now leave him
> alone. Let's see if Elijah comes to take him down," he
> said. (Mark 15:36)

In Jewish legend, Elijah was celebrated as one who helped those in need, so the man steps back and waits for the show to begin.

The man has a sort of superstitious fascination as he contemplates the cross. He offers Jesus a sponge filled with wine vinegar, presumably to help postpone an inevitable death, but nothing in the scene moves him to awe, reverence, or even pity. He just wants to experiment while Jesus dies.

Just before he died, the writer Kingsley Amis said this in an interview with the Daily Telegraph:

> One of Christianity's great advantages is that it offers an
> explanation for sin. I haven't got one. Christianity's got
> one enormous thing right – original sin – for one of the
> great benefits of organised religion is that you can be
> forgiven your sins, which must be a wonderful thing.

The interviewer records that here Amis bowed his head and said, "I mean, I carry my sins around with me. There's nobody to forgive them."

For whatever reason, Kingsley Amis remained a spectator while Jesus Christ was offering him the one thing he craved most. The curtain has been torn from top to bottom, the way is open to God, but the spectator walks away from the cross unchanged.

Some people think it's fine to be a bystander. Some do it by coming to church every Christmas and Easter, enjoying the ceremony and tradition, and then leaving unmoved. Others do it because they think there's no need to do anything in the light of Jesus' death, as if even spectators automatically receive the benefit. But the truth is that I only benefit from the death of Jesus if I put my trust in him. Again, the bystander walks away from the foot of the cross, blind to the true significance of what they've just witnessed.

By recording all these reactions, Mark is telling us that no one can remain neutral when they consider the cross. We are either too busy like the soldiers, too self-satisfied like the religious, too cowardly like Pilate, or too detached like the bystander.

Actually, there is one last possible reaction to the cross. This response, made by the Roman centurion, is the culmination of everything we've read so far.

Reaction Five: The Roman centurion
He is a hard-bitten Roman soldier, the equivalent of a Regimental Sergeant Major, a veteran in charge of a hundred men. He has doubtless fought many gruelling campaigns and seen many men die, but he has never seen a man die like this:

> ... when the centurion, who stood there in front of Jesus,
> heard his cry and saw how he died, he said, "Surely this
> man was the Son of God!"

Despite being one of those responsible for carrying out the execution, the centurion acknowledges Jesus to be the Son of God. His words echo the very first words of Mark's Gospel – "the gospel about Jesus Christ, the Son of God". And that is our final possibility as we look at what happened at the cross. We can recognize that Jesus is telling the truth. That he is indeed the Son of God.

Looking across London's skyline, you can see the home of British justice, the Old Bailey. On top of the building is Pomeroy's magnificent golden statue of Lady Justice. In one hand she is holding the scales of justice and in the other she holds the sword of wrath. It's a reminder that no matter who we are, if we are found to be guilty, the sword of wrath must fall.

If you then let your gaze wander across the skyline a short distance you'll find another golden object, this time at the top of St Paul's cathedral. It's a cross, a reminder that although the sword of wrath must fall, it fell on Jesus Christ. In that moment our indignant cries for justice were perfectly satisfied and our desperate calls for God's mercy were lovingly answered. And in the light of that, what should I do with my sin?

Will I take it to the cross to be forgiven, or will I take it with me to my grave, and to the judgment that must fall?

5.
MORNING WILL COME

Being reunited with someone you love is one of the happiest experiences on earth. The familiar face, the comforting voice, the reassuring embrace. But there are some separations, as we know to our cost, which last much longer.

Recently I read the story of a well-known Christian theologian who was on a plane heading toward the east coast of the United States. He got talking to the passenger in the next seat, a pastor from Texas, and the conversation turned to family.

The theologian told the pastor how he had recently lost his four-year old son to a terrible illness. It began innocently enough when the child was sent home from school one afternoon after developing a fever. At first the parents thought it was a typical childhood illness that would soon run its course. But his condition continued to worsen and that evening they took him to the hospital.

The doctors ran a battery of tests and told the parents tragic news – their son had a virulent form of meningitis and there was nothing they could do for him. The child was beyond their help and was going to die.

The loving parents did the only thing they could do, which was sit with their son in a death vigil.

It was the middle of the afternoon, only a few days after he became sick, and the illness was causing the little boy's vision to fade. He looked up at his daddy and said softly, "Daddy, it's getting dark, isn't it?"

The professor replied, "Yes, son, it is dark. It's very dark." And for the father it was.

The little boy said, "I guess it's time for me to get to sleep, isn't it?"

"Yes son, it's time for you to sleep," said the father.

The theologian explained... how his son liked his pillow and his blankets arranged just so and that he laid his head on his hands while he slept. He told how he helped the child fix his pillow and how his little boy rested his head on his hands and said, "Good night daddy. I'll see you in the morning." With that the little boy closed his eyes and fell asleep. Only a few minutes later his little chest rose and fell for the last time and his life was over almost before it began.

The professor stopped talking and looked out the window of the aeroplane for a good long time. Finally he turned... and with his voice breaking and tears spilling onto his cheeks gasped, "I can hardly wait for morning to come..."[9]

As you hear that story, do you dismiss it as the wishful thinking of a grieving parent? Or could it be true that one

---

9 Tim Challies, *Snapshots and Screenshots*, p28-29, http://www.challies.com/articles/snapshots-screenshots (accessed 7th July 2011)

day, the long hoped-for morning will actually come?

The promise of Jesus Christ, signed in his blood and sealed by his resurrection, is that it will. Although premature darkness came across the land that Friday afternoon, although they watched his chest rise and fall for the last time, the broken-hearted friends would be reunited with Jesus again. Not in some imaginary, sentimental, non-physical way. But in flesh and blood reality. Their morning would come.

But what evidence is there that the physical resurrection of Jesus – and one day, of us – is more than wishful thinking?

The death was certain

To be sure that Jesus really did rise from death, we have to be sure that he really died in the first place. Mark calls as witnesses three women who watched him die, the Roman governor Pontius Pilate, the Roman centurion who also watched him die, and Joseph of Arimathea, a prominent member of the Jewish council, who personally wrapped Jesus' body in linen and placed it in a tomb.

First of all, at the end of his account of the crucifixion in chapter 15, Mark homes in on three women who have watched the whole blood-soaked execution:

> Some women were watching [the crucifixion] from a
> distance. Among them were Mary Magdalene, Mary the
> mother of James the younger and of Joses, and Salome.
> In Galilee these women had followed him and cared for
> his needs. Many other women who had come up with him
> to Jerusalem were also there.

Not only have they watched Jesus die, but two of them also watch him being buried: "Mary Magdalene and Mary the mother of Joses saw where he was laid." They are firsthand witnesses of his death, and when they return later to the tomb, they bring with them spices – spices which were used to anoint a dead body.

Mark goes on to tell us:

> It was Preparation Day (that is, the day before the Sabbath). So as evening approached, Joseph of Arimathea, a prominent member of the Council, who was himself waiting for the kingdom of God, went boldly to Pilate and asked for Jesus' body. Pilate was surprised to hear that he was already dead. Summoning the centurion, he asked him if Jesus had already died. When he learned from the centurion that it was so, he gave the body to Joseph.

It was unusual for crucifixion to result in death so quickly, so the Roman governor Pontius Pilate queries the centurion, presumably the same centurion who had stood only a short distance from the cross and watched the extraordinary way in which Jesus had died. The centurion confirms that yes, Jesus had indeed already died.

The Romans had many talents, but when it came to killing people, they were experts. In chapter 19 of John's Gospel, we're told that because it was the day before their holy day, the Jewish authorities did not want bodies left on crosses.

As a result, they ask Pilate to have the legs of the condemned broken in order to hasten their deaths (the only way you can breathe on a cross is if you keep pushing yourself up with your legs). Soldiers are duly despatched to carry out the order, and it's worth remembering that failure to do so would have meant facing execution themselves. So they break the legs of the two criminals crucified with Jesus.

But when they come to Jesus they find that he is "already dead"; there is no need to break any bones "Instead," we are told, "one of the soldiers pierced Jesus' side with a spear, bringing a sudden flow of blood and water." Why bother lancing him in this way? Perhaps it was sheer brutality but, whatever the reason, the "flow of blood and water" also suggests that Jesus was dead: the blood coagulates when we die, leaving the water to separate away from the blood. (Incidentally, the fact that Jesus would not have any bones broken – an extremely unusual fact given these circumstances – is anticipated in sections of the Bible written hundreds of years previously.[10])

Having firmly established that Jesus is dead, Pilate gives Joseph permission to remove the body from the cross:

> So Joseph bought some linen cloth, took down the body, wrapped it in the linen, and placed it in a tomb cut out of rock. Then he rolled a stone against the entrance of the tomb.

> (Incidentally, John 19:38-42 describes how Joseph and another man called Nicodemus prepare Jesus for burial:

---

10 See Psalm 34:20. Another example is Exodus 12:46, where God tells his people that the lamb given as a sacrifice for their sin must not have any of its bones broken.

"Nicodemus brought a mixture of myrrh and aloes, about seventy-five pounds. Taking Jesus' body, the two of them wrapped it, with the spices, in strips of linen. This was in accordance with Jewish burial customs.")

Mark is very clear: the women, Pontius Pilate, the centurion, and Joseph of Arimathea were all absolutely convinced that Jesus had died.

The tomb was empty

We are told in Matthew's Gospel that on the next day (Saturday, the Sabbath), in addition to the large stone placed over the entrance, a seal was placed upon the tomb. (This was because some of the religious leaders feared that the disciples would steal the body and then pretend that Jesus had come back from the dead.) People knew that to break such a seal resulted in execution. Further security was provided in the form of carefully trained guards, deployed to ensure that no one tampered with the tomb.

Once the Jewish holy day is over, the women return to the tomb that they had watched Jesus being buried in just 36 hours earlier. As we've seen, they don't go hoping that Jesus might be alive, they go expecting to find a corpse. Mark chapter 16 verses 1 to 3:

When the Sabbath was over, Mary Magdalene, Mary the mother of James, and Salome bought spices so that they might go to anoint Jesus' body. Very early on the first day of the week, just after sunrise, they were on their way to the tomb and they asked each other, "Who will roll the stone away from the entrance of the tomb?"

And then the women are subjected to three shocks of escalating intensity.

The first shock comes when they find that their concern over who will roll the stone away is irrelevant:

> But when they looked up, they saw that the stone, which was very large, had been rolled away.

There is no need to fret about the stone, because divine power has dealt with it. Then comes the second shock, as they go inside the tomb:

> As they entered the tomb, they saw a young man dressed in a white robe sitting on the right side, and they were alarmed.

They see a man whose appearance is so striking ("like lightning", according to Matthew) that it causes the guards posted to the tomb to shake (Matthew tells us that they become "like dead men"). The women, understandably, are terrified. But they are not delusional – the man affirms the reality of what is happening:

> "Don't be alarmed," he said. "You are looking for Jesus the Nazarene, who was crucified."

Yes, the man from Nazareth, the one you've been following these past three years, really was killed.

> See the place where they laid him.

Yes, he really was buried here, you haven't accidentally gone to the wrong tomb. The fact is that Jesus simply isn't here any more. As for the guards' reaction, Matthew tells us this:

...some of the guards went into the city and reported to
the chief priests everything that had happened. When
the chief priests had met with the elders and devised a
plan, they gave the soldiers a large sum of money, telling
them, "You are to say, 'His disciples came during the
night and stole him away while we were asleep.' If this
report gets to the governor, we will satisfy him and keep
you out of trouble." So the soldiers took the money and
did as they were instructed.[11]

But the third shock will change the women's lives forever.

The body was resurrected

This third shock, the biggest of them all, comes as the
young man in the empty tomb tells them the reason why
Jesus' body is not there:

He has risen! (Mark 16:6)

Just as there was no need for their concern about the
stone, there is now no need for the spices they'd brought
to anoint the corpse. Divine power has not only flung
the stone away, it has raised a body to life. The reason
the tomb is empty is because Jesus isn't dead any more.
He is alive.

But go, tell his disciples and Peter, 'He is going ahead of
you into Galilee. There you will see him, just as he told you.

The one they thought was lost to them forever, the one
they thought they would never see again, was waiting
to be reunited with them in Galilee. In the place they

---

11 Matthew 28:11-15

first met him, where everything started. Their morning had come.

Dr Simon Greenleaf, the celebrated Royal Professor of Law at Harvard University, who was famously sceptical of Christianity, was challenged to evaluate the resurrection of Jesus using well-established legal principles. He wrote this:

> According to the laws of legal evidence, the resurrection of Jesus Christ is proven by more substantial evidence than any other event of ancient history.[12]

Other biblical accounts tell us there were at least ten separate occasions when Jesus appeared to his disciples after his death. Remarkably, we also read that more than five hundred people saw him at the same time.[13] So this was no ghost or hallucination, seen fleetingly by one or two unreliable individuals. Jesus actually had a physical body that could eat and drink, be talked to and touched.

As the years passed, all except one of the disciples joyfully and peacefully suffered violent executions simply because they knew beyond any doubt that Jesus was indeed raised from death. They had seen it with their own eyes, and no threat or torture could make them deny what they knew was true.

They had seen firsthand that Jesus had triumphed over death – so death no longer had any fear for them, or any power over them. We sometimes hear of people dying for a lie they believe is true. But when is the last

---

12 Simon Greenleaf, *The Testimony of the Evangelists: The Four Gospels Examined by the Rules of Evidence* (Grand Rapids: Kregel Publications, 1995).
13 1 Corinthians 15:6

time you heard of someone dying for a "truth" they know is a lie?

In fact, one of the most striking pieces of evidence that Jesus' followers actually met the resurrected Jesus is their otherwise inexplicable transformation from fearful into fearless. At first, they were anything but fearless. In Mark chapter 16, Mark records the way in which the women react to the empty tomb:

> Trembling and bewildered, the women went out and fled from the tomb. They said nothing to anyone, because they were afraid. (Mark 16:8)

Even though Jesus had told them repeatedly in advance that it was all part of the plan, it's still too much for them to fully understand or accept. And it may be that it's a struggle for you too. Our temptation may be to forget all the evidence we've seen about who Jesus is, and what he said he would do. Like the women, our instinct may be to run away from the resurrection, and say nothing to anyone.

But remember the words of the young man in the tomb. He told the women to tell the disciples:

> He is going ahead of you into Galilee. There you will see him, just as he told you. (Mark 16:7)

The resurrection promises not only that the disciples will see the risen Jesus. One day, "you will see him" too.

You will see him
Acts 17 verse 31 tells us:

> For he [God] has set a day when he will judge the world with justice by the man he has appointed. He has given

proof of this to all men by raising him from the dead.

In other words, the resurrection is the guarantee that everyone who has ever lived will one day be raised to life, and justly judged by Jesus himself. The only question is, are we ready to meet him?

One man who certainly was not ready was Peter, the fisherman from Galilee who had been one of Jesus' closest disciples, the one who guided Mark as he wrote his book. Peter was the disciple who had earlier criticized Jesus for predicting his own death and resurrection. Who had fallen asleep when Jesus had told him to keep watch. Who had told Jesus, "Even if I have to die with you, I will never disown you", and then, that same night, had denied even knowing Jesus. Not once, but three times.

We know that Peter felt the terrible weight of his own sin. Mark tells us that as soon as he disowned Jesus for the third time...

> Peter remembered the word Jesus had spoken to him: "Before the cock crows twice you will disown me three times." And he broke down and wept. (Mark 14:72)

Peter wept because he knew his sin had finally caught up with him. And there was nothing he could do to put it right.

But remember the words spoken by the man in the empty tomb, after Jesus is raised:

> Go, tell his disciples and Peter, "He is going ahead of you into Galilee. There you will see him, just as he told you." (Mark 16:7)

"And Peter" is such a beautiful phrase. Having died to

pay for sin, and having risen from death to prove that sin was truly paid for, Jesus wants Peter to know that he is included. Even Peter, with all his doubt and stubbornness, failure and weakness. If he would simply trust Jesus, then every sin – every denial, every failure to love God as he should – would be fully and finally forgiven. The friends would be reunited.

One of the first funerals I ever took was for a professional musician called Stuart Spencer, who died of leukaemia in his late thirties. I saw him three days before he died, and I'll always remember my last visit to him. I was feeling emotional and without thinking I just said, "Stuart, what's it like to die?" (It was one of those moments where you think to yourself, "Did I just say that out loud?")

I'll never forget his answer. He looked at me very calmly and said, "Rico, Christ has risen. The resurrection may be precious to you, but I'm going to stand before God in a few days' time. Do you have any idea how precious it is to me?"

You see, Stuart knew he was a sinner – just like Peter, just like you and me. But he also knew for certain that Christ had died and risen for sinners. And because of that, he knew what awaited him beyond death: a real, physical resurrection of his body, a body that would eat and drink, be talked to and touched. A body that would never again see sorrow or suffering, disease or decay.

He also knew who awaited him, ready to welcome him. The familiar face, the comforting voice, the reassuring embrace. Because of the resurrection, Stuart knew that the morning would come.

6.
NO NEED TO EARN IT

If God were to say to you, "Why should I give you eternal life?", what would you say?

I've asked hundreds of people that question over the years, but the answers tend to be along similar lines: "I don't steal. I don't lie. I give to charity. I'm quite a spiritual person. I try to treat others as I like to be treated myself. I've been baptized. I go to church. I go to communion. I read the Bible. I'm basically a good person. That's why God should give me eternal life." One person even said to me, "Rico, I give blood. I give blood!"

But is that enough?

Earn it

The film *Saving Private Ryan*, set during World War II, tells the story of how a single man – Private James Ryan – was rescued from behind enemy lines in Normandy. Early in the film, we're told that his three brothers have all recently been killed in action, leaving James Ryan as the only child of a single mother. Hearing of this situation, the US Army Chief of Staff gives orders to protect this precious remaining son, and he sends out a team of soldiers to bring him back alive.

The rescue mission is extremely perilous, and one after another, it starts claiming the lives of the soldiers. At one point the Captain leading the mission says, "This Ryan had better be worth it. He'd better go home, cure some disease or invent the longer-lasting light bulb."

But the rescue team presses on. And in the final battle scene, set on a heavily-shelled bridge, as the Captain himself dies, he whispers his last words to a dumbstruck Private Ryan: "James – earn this – earn it".

For many of us, that is the only way we can save ourselves. Somehow, whether it be through religious practice or by trying to be " a good person", we live our whole lives trying to "earn it".

The rich young ruler

The so-called "rich young ruler" of Mark chapter 10 is very much like that. He's worked hard all his life to "earn it". He's what you might call "a good person".

Two other writers in the Bible tell us about the same event, and together with Mark they help us build up a picture of what this man was like. It's Matthew who tells us that the man was young, while Luke adds the detail that the man was a "ruler" of some kind. And it's clear from Mark that he was rich, morally upright, spiritually-minded, and very religious.

So he has everything going for him. He's young, he's rich and he's powerful. And to those who knew him, he would have been very well respected. In other words, he's exactly the sort of person many of us would like to be.

But there's also a vulnerability about him. He runs up to Jesus, falls on his knees in the dirt – which in my experience is typically not something rich people do – and asks Jesus a question. It's the most important question anyone could ask:

> "Good teacher," he asked, "what must I do to inherit eternal life?" (Mark 10:17)

"Inherit eternal life" is another way of saying "enter the kingdom of God" or "have treasure in heaven" or "be saved". All these phrases are used in Mark 10 to mean a similar thing: the overwhelming joy of being forgiven and accepted by God himself, free to enjoy him forever – in this life, and the life to come. What must I do, says the man, to get that? How can I be good enough?

Good enough for God?

Jesus asks a question straight back.

> "Why do you call me good?" Jesus answered. "No one is good — except God alone." (Mark 10:18)

This is Jesus offering the man a reality check. In effect, he is asking him, "Just how good is good enough for God?"

I wonder how you'd answer that question. Many of us would instinctively say, "Well, I know I'm not perfect, but on the whole, I'm a pretty good person." We think of ourselves as basically good because we tend to compare ourselves to other flawed human beings. It's easy to imagine ourselves in a favourable light if we only see ourselves in relation to certain people on TV, people we don't like, or people we secretly look down on.

But Jesus is saying, if you want to know who really deserves to be called good, who really deserves to inherit eternal life, try comparing yourself to God – who alone is perfectly just, perfectly wise, perfectly pure and perfectly loving. Then you'll get a sense of how good you really are.

But the man doesn't get it. So Jesus continues:

> "You know the commandments: 'Do not murder, do not commit adultery, do not steal, do not give false testimony, do not defraud, honour your father and mother.'"
> "Teacher," he declared, "all these I have kept since I was a boy." (Mark 10:19-20)

If God were to say to this man, "Why should I give you eternal life?", that's the answer the man would give: "I've kept all your commands since I was a boy."

But has he? Jesus, patiently and lovingly, gives the man another reality check:

> Jesus looked at him and loved him. "One thing you lack," he said. "Go, sell everything you have and give to the poor, and you will have treasure in heaven.
> Then come, follow me." (Mark 10:21)

Has the man really kept all God's commands? Is he even keeping what Jesus calls the first and most important command, to love the Lord your God with all your heart, soul, mind and strength?[14] To see if he really does love

---

14 Mark 12: 28-31. In fact, as we're about to see, when the man refuses to give to the poor, he is also breaking what Jesus calls the second most important command: to "love your neighbour as yourself."

God like that, Jesus tests the man with a challenge: "Give your money away."

And suddenly, the young man is feeling much less certain of himself:

> At this the man's face fell. (Mark 10:22)

It reminds me of the famous old joke. A robber goes up to a rich man, points a gun at him and says, "Your money or your life." But the rich man does nothing. So the robber shouts even louder: "I'm not kidding, your money or your life!" And the man (after a long pause) looks at him and says, "I'm thinking, I'm thinking!"

Money or life. It should be a no-brainer. Which one will the rich young man choose?

> He went away sad, because he had great wealth.
> (Mark 10:22)

Now can I say as clearly as I can that this is not Jesus teaching that his followers should give all their money to the church. That is not what this is about. Instead, Jesus wants the man (and you and I) to reflect on what is most important to us. Are we really loving God more than anything else? Or do we love someone – or something – more?

Faced with the choice between holding on to his money or gaining eternal life, this man chooses money. The fact that he walks away from Jesus at this point shows that, although he thinks of himself as a good person, in reality he loves money more than he loves God. He has broken what Jesus calls the first and most important commandment of all.

I wonder what it would be for us. What is the one thing you would not be willing to let go of, the one thing that would keep you from gaining the eternal life that Jesus is holding out to you? Our answer to that question reveals how far we are from good, and how far we are from God.

"With man this is impossible"

> Jesus looked around and said to his disciples, "How
> hard it is for the rich to enter the kingdom of God!" The
> disciples were amazed at his words. But Jesus said again,
> "Children, how hard it is to enter the kingdom of God!
> It is easier for a camel to go through the eye of a needle
> than for a rich man to enter the kingdom of God."
> (Mark 10:23-25)

In other words, it's impossible.

The disciples are amazed because money was seen as a blessing from God; they understood it to mean that God was pleased with a person. But Jesus is saying that even a morally upright, thoroughly religious, politically powerful, exceptionally wealthy young man can never do enough good things to enter the kingdom of God. Why? Because nothing we do, nothing we are, can change the fact that deep down, all of us have a serious heart problem. And that means we can never be good enough for God.

As we've already seen, Jesus exposes the real state of our hearts when he says:

> What comes out of a man is what makes him "unclean."
> For from within, out of men's hearts, come evil thoughts,

sexual immorality, theft, murder, adultery, greed, malice,
deceit, lewdness, envy, slander, arrogance and folly. All
these evils come from inside and make a man "unclean".
(Mark 7:20-23)

It is what we are. Deep down at the very core of our being.

When I was young I went on a rugby tour, and while we were travelling I got this awful skin disease which made my face look not unlike a cheese and tomato pizza. So I started putting Band-Aids on my face, little sticky plasters to cover up these horrible sores that made people sick at the sight of me.

Now, the plasters helped to cover up the fact that something was wrong with me, but of course they were powerless to cure the disease. For that, the doctor had to prescribe some industrial-strength antibiotics to get at the infection deep in my bloodstream.

In the same way, the things we do to try and make ourselves good enough – the things we do to try and "earn it" – are like sticking plasters or Band-Aids. They may cover up the fact that there's a problem deep down in our hearts. They may make other people think we're pretty good people. We may even fool ourselves.

But these things we do – all the religion, all the morality – are completely powerless to cure the problem of our sin. Any answer that begins, "God, you should give me eternal life because I...", any answer which places confidence in anything you are or anything you have done will not be of any use. Again, let me say as clearly as I can that according to Jesus, these things will not enable you to inherit eternal life.

If you're putting your trust in any of these things, please don't, because you've been misled.

Regardless of how moral or good we think we are, we fail to obey even the very first command, the most important command: love the Lord your God with all your heart, soul, mind and strength. Like the man, our hearts love other things more. And that is what separates us – forever – from God.

The disciples understand immediately that this leaves each of us in a desperate situation. If a rich man can't make it into the kingdom of God, then who on earth can?

> The disciples were even more amazed, and said to each other, "Who then can be saved?" (Mark 10:26)

And Jesus' answer is devastating.

> Jesus looked at them and said, "With man this is impossible..." (Mark 10:27)

In other words, there are some things we will never deserve, can never earn, and should never even try to pay for. It is impossible for us to be saved by "earning it".

"...But not with God."
But that doesn't mean we can't receive something as a gift from God. Jesus continues:

> With man this is impossible, *but not with God*; all things are possible with God. (Mark 10:27, my italics)

So how can any of us inherit eternal life if there is nothing we can do to inherit it? Strangely enough, if the rich young man had arrived only a short while earlier, he would have heard Jesus answer exactly that question.

Immediately before this encounter, Jesus meets some people who are the exact opposite of the rich young man. Where he has material things, they have nothing. Where he is well respected, they are overlooked. Where he has power, they are so weak they have to be brought to Jesus. And where he walks away sadly from Jesus, they cling to him.

> People were bringing little children to Jesus to have him touch them, but the disciples rebuked them. When Jesus saw this, he was indignant. He said to them, "Let the little children come to me, and do not hinder them, for the kingdom of God belongs to such as these. I tell you the truth, anyone who will not receive the kingdom of God like a little child will never enter it." And he took the children in his arms, put his hands on them and blessed them. (Mark 10:13-16)

By speaking of little children, Jesus isn't saying we have to be naive or gullible to inherit the kingdom of God. And he isn't talking about innocence or purity here. Having been one myself, innocence is not a quality I'd associate with a little child.

The quality little children have that Jesus commends to us is their dependency. They depend on someone else to do everything for them, because they know they can do nothing for themselves. All they can do is throw out their arms and cry for help.

Small children don't try to pay for their meals, or a place to sleep, or the love that their parents show them, because they can't. They have no way of paying and they can't earn it. They are totally dependent. They must receive everything as a gift. They must trust that it will all be done for them by someone else. And that, says Jesus, is the only way anyone can enter the kingdom of God.

Do you see how this makes the message of Jesus very different from the message of other religions? Other faiths say that, if you do certain things, and don't do other things, then God will accept you. But Jesus tells us that that is simply not true. Because the problem of the human heart is so serious, the only way we can ever hope to be accepted by God is if he reaches out to us, pays the price for our sin himself, and then offers us forgiveness as a gift. And that is exactly what happened when he sent Jesus to die on the cross in our place.

We can't earn it and we don't deserve it. In fact, we deserve the opposite – God's punishment. And yet Jesus took that punishment on our behalf, so that all those who put their trust in him would be freely forgiven.

If you want to enter the kingdom of God, says Jesus, if you want to experience the overwhelming joy of being forgiven and accepted by God himself, welcomed into the intimacy of his own family, free to enjoy him forever – in this life, and the life to come – if you want that, the only way to do it is to accept it as a child would accept it: knowing you have no way of earning it or deserving it, content simply to receive it joyfully as a gift. All we can do is come to him. Not with hands filled with all the things we have done, but with empty hands. Ready to receive what God has done.

The great exchange

At the end of *Saving Private Ryan*, there is a scene set fifty years after the Captain died rescuing James Ryan. We see an elderly James Ryan returning to Normandy with his wife, children and grandchildren.

He kneels beside the grave of the Captain and, as tears fill his eyes, he says, "My family is with me today... Every day I think about what you said to me that day on the bridge. ("Earn it!") I've tried to live my life the best I could. I hope that was enough. I hope that at least in your eyes I've earned what all of you have done for me." Then he turns to his wife with some anxiety and pleads with her, "Tell me I've led a good life... Tell me I'm a good man..."

Private Ryan has lived his entire life with the last words of his rescuer ringing in his ears. "Earn this – earn it." In a way, the words have crippled him. How could he ever live up to the deaths of those young men who gave their lives to rescue him?

The words the Captain cried out just before he died were "Earn it". But the words Jesus cried out just before he died were very different:

> My God, my God, why have you forsaken me?
> (Mark 15:34)

They, too, are words that will alter the course of a person's life. Because the way we answer that question will change us forever. Why was Jesus forsaken?

We've already seen the answer earlier in Mark. The reason God the Father forsakes God the Son at the cross is because he was dying "as a ransom for many". He was paying the price for people like us, people like the rich young man, who have constantly failed to obey even the first, and most important, commandment: love the Lord your God with all your heart, soul, mind and strength.

But Jesus achieved even more than that. By living the perfectly loving life we are incapable of living, he was "earning it" for us. He lived as we would have to live if we were to inherit eternal life by our own efforts.

2 Corinthians chapter 5 verse 21 puts it like this:

> God made him who had no sin to be sin for us, so that in him we might become the righteousness of God.

Do you see what Jesus has done? Jesus took upon himself all our sin, so that we can take upon ourselves his righteousness. When God looks at us – if we've put our trust in Jesus – he sees the perfect obedience, the perfect love, the perfect righteousness of his Son.

And that's what grace is. It's God behaving towards us in a way we simply do not deserve. When we look at Jesus' life and death, we see God graciously reaching out to us, offering us something that we have not – and cannot possibly – earn. It's something that must simply be received, not as a reward, but as a gift paid for by God himself. Jesus "earned it" for us, at the cross.

How grace can change you

When someone who doesn't know you at all tells you you're loved, it might be nice, but the feeling doesn't last very long.

But when a spouse or a best friend who knows you well tells you how loved you are, it makes you feel wonderful.

Imagine then what it means when the Creator of the universe, who knows you better than anyone, shows you that he loves you so much, he would die on your behalf. It is the most precious gift anyone could possibly receive. Rather than being crippled by the demand to "earn it", we experience the breathtaking joy and freedom that comes from being told that Jesus has already earned it for us.

God knows all about our sinful hearts, but when we put our trust in Jesus, God loves us as deeply and relentlessly as he loves his Son.

So we no longer need to pretend we're something we're not. We get our sense of worth from God's love for us. We're freed from the slavery of constantly trying to get our sense of worth from all the other places we – just like the rich young man – have tried to earn it: money or power, religiousness or career, good looks or the approval of others. It also means that we – unlike James Ryan – no longer have to live our lives under the heavy and hopeless burden of trying to earn our way into God's kingdom.

When you come to Jesus, you understand just how loved you are by God. When you look at the cross it's as if Jesus is saying, "This is what it costs to earn that gift for you. This is how serious your sin really is. And this is how much I love you anyway." We are more sinful than we ever realized, but more loved than we ever dreamed.

Imagine how you would feel if an earthly king said to you, "Everything I am is now yours. Everything I have is now yours. I will take care of you from now on. If you are ever in danger, I will take care of you. If you ever need anything, I will meet your deepest needs." It would be stunning. We would be overjoyed. All our discontent would be swallowed up in a second.

And that is the gift the King is holding out to you now.

"Come to me with empty hands," says Jesus. "There's something I want you to have."

7.
A STORY OF SEEDS

So far, as we've explored the life of Jesus, we've looked at who he is and why he came. The question now is, how should we respond?

As we're about to see, Jesus in effect says: if you come to me, it will be truly and miraculously life-changing. But you have to listen to me for that to happen.

Surprisingly for a man of his great power and authority, Jesus tells a story which likens the extraordinary, life-changing power of his words to tiny, vulnerable seeds.

His point is this: just as seeds will only grow if you plant them properly, so the good news about Jesus will only change your life if you hear it properly. Here's the story, as Jesus tells it in Mark chapter 4:

> "Listen! A farmer went out to sow his seed. As he was scattering the seed, some fell along the path, and the birds came and ate it up. Some fell on rocky places, where it did not have much soil. It sprang up quickly, because the soil was shallow. But when the sun came up, the plants were scorched, and they withered because they had no root. Other seed fell among thorns, which

grew up and choked the plants, so that they did not bear
grain. Still other seed fell on good soil. It came up, grew
and produced a crop, multiplying thirty, sixty, or even a
hundred times."
Then Jesus said, "He who has ears to hear, let him hear."
(Mark 4:3-9)

I don't know if you realized it, but you had a walk-on part in that story. Everyone who has ever heard the good news, the gospel about Jesus, appears in it. It's as if Jesus is holding up a mirror so that we can see ourselves reflected back.

Because, although this story is usually called "The Parable of the Sower", the main focus is not on the sower. Or the seed. As you may have noticed, Jesus' focus is on the soil, because every person who hears Jesus' words – and every person who reads this chapter – is a different kind of "soil". Each one of us receives the good news about Jesus in a different way.

And quite deliberately, at this point in our exploration of Mark's Gospel, Jesus is very pointedly asking us the question, "How are you responding to the gospel? What kind of soil are you?" According to Jesus, there are four possibilities.

The vulnerable soil

Some people are like seed along the path, where the
word is sown. As soon as they hear it, Satan comes and
takes away the word that was sown in them. (Mark 4:15)

The fields in ancient Israel were long, narrow strips divided by little paths. Over the years, the constant traffic of footsteps, hooves and wheels turned these paths as hard as concrete. So if seeds fell here, they'd never go deep into the soil, they'd just bounce off and remain on the surface. The seed would become food for birds.

Quite unapologetically, Jesus says that the birds who come and snatch up the seeds in the story are a picture of Satan, whose aim is always to stop the gospel from being properly heard – immediately if possible.

There's a sign near my home that says, "Thieves operate in this area. You don't have to be a victim. Guard your valuables." And it's a very similar message to the one Jesus gives here. Satan is a reality, warns Jesus. He's like a thief who wants to rob you of something far more valuable than your wallet or purse. He wants to rob you of the gospel.

And there's nothing worse than discovering that you've been robbed without even knowing it. You don't even realize that you're missing something until much later. But that's what happens here. Before the gospel even registers in the person's mind, something comes to snatch it away. This person may be a hardened sceptic who immediately rejects anything that will challenge their own ideas, or it may simply be someone who is easily distracted. As soon as the Bible is closed, the words are forgotten.

But, as we'll see in a moment, "You don't have to be a victim".

The shallow soil

> Others, like seed sown on rocky places, hear the word
> and at once receive it with joy. But since they have
> no root, they last only a short time. When trouble or

> persecution comes because of the word, they quickly fall
> away. (Mark 4:16-17)

In Israel, some of the land has a thin two- or three-inch layer of soil lying on top of the limestone bedrock. If seed falls there, the sun heats the soil quickly because it's so shallow, and the seed immediately sprouts up. In the short run, this soil looks like the best kind of soil. The immediate growth is spectacular. But the bedrock only a few inches below means there's nothing for the roots to go down into, and no way for the plant to get moisture. So it quickly dies.

I must be honest: I love books, but I have a terrible habit of starting one, getting into it, and then leaving it unfinished while I start another one. And some people have the same issue with the gospel. They start with real eagerness. They seem truly excited about getting to know Christ. But then the early excitement fades. Because of their interest in Jesus, friends, family and people at work start cutting them out of the conversation, keeping them at arm's length – or, in some parts of the world, far, far worse.

And at that point, the person decides it's easier to give up on Jesus than put up with the discomfort. The Christian life gets discarded. They haven't thought through what it means to follow him, the cost of being for what he is for, and against what he is against. Their desire to know him is revealed as shallow and short-lived, and they're not grounded enough to persevere.

The thorny soil

> Still others, like seed sown among thorns, hear the word;
> but the worries of this life, the deceitfulness of wealth
> and the desires for other things come in and choke the
> word, making it unfruitful. (Mark 4:18-19)

At first the plant seems to be doing well. But it can't compete with the thorns which grow up alongside it.

It's like the story of the young man who said, "Darling, I want you to know that I love you more than anything else in the world. Will you marry me? I know I'm not rich, I don't have a big house or a beautiful car like Jeffrey Brown, but I do love you with all my heart."

And the young woman replies, "I love you with all my heart too. But just a moment – tell me more about Jeffrey Brown."

And it's the same for the third type of person in the parable. Somehow they let their desire for other things become competition for their involvement with Jesus. Their hearts are divided. Desire for security, comfort, approval or power, maybe money, maybe the desire for a potential spouse who doesn't share their view of Jesus – these desires, and the worries that come with them, become stronger than the desire for Jesus.

This person doesn't see that the security, comfort, approval and power that come from knowing Christ infinitely outweigh any treasure the world has to offer.

But there is a fourth and final type of soil.

The good soil

> Others, like seed sown on good soil, hear the word,
> accept it, and produce a crop — thirty, sixty or even a
> hundred times what was sown. (Mark 4:20)

This type of growth is out of the ordinary. Even modern farming methods can't produce the kind of huge crop Jesus describes here. He wants us to understand that something supernatural is happening.

When the gospel is heard by someone who truly hears it and does what it says, something miraculous happens, something that cannot be accounted for in human terms. And it happens when the person hearing the gospel sees Jesus for who he is, understands why he came, and what it means to follow him. It happens when they understand that Jesus is the greatest treasure in the world.

When I was younger, I used to get a comic delivered by mail. It always arrived on a Tuesday just after breakfast, but because I had to go to school, I didn't get a chance to read it until break time. I remember reaching into my satchel, just to touch it, to remind myself that it was there. And when break time came, I used to run out of class as if it was on fire and go somewhere I wouldn't be disturbed. Sometimes I ended up perched in the branches of a tree, and other times I locked myself in a cubicle in the boys' room. Either way, nothing could be allowed to stop me from reading that week's edition of my favourite comic.

Nothing.

Now the surroundings weren't the most comfortable, but I was completely absorbed and content as I opened my bag to read my comic. Nothing else mattered. Why? Because I had my treasure. It was all I wanted or needed.

When Jesus talks about the good soil, he's talking about someone who not only hears the gospel about Jesus Christ, but makes it their treasure. When Jesus himself becomes more valuable to you than anything else in the world, when nothing else matters to you as much as he does, that's when you know you've truly heard him.

The powerful seed

There may be areas of your heart you think are impenetrable and unreachable. There may be self-image issues, battles with addiction or alienation or abuse. You may feel trapped by all kinds of darkness inside you, things you feel you can't even admit. Let Jesus' story give you hope. His words, though they may seem small and vulnerable, become stunningly powerful when we apply them to our own lives.

I remember the story of a man who visited a cemetery in Italy. He said he noticed a thick marble slab over the top of one of the graves. But somehow, about a hundred years earlier, an acorn had fallen through a small crack into the grave.

And over the years the acorn had grown and grown until eventually it had smashed through the surface of the hard marble and cracked the enormous slab into two pieces. As the tree grew up, it just pushed the marble aside as if it wasn't there. There is enormous power packed into a tiny seed. All it needed was the right kind of soil.

The good news about Jesus, though it may seem small and weak, has the power to break through and transform any human heart – if only we will listen and act on what we hear.

The word of God doesn't come to us so that we can give the right answers to religious questions. It comes to us because God wants us to be in relationship with him. The gospel tells us that Jesus Christ has fully paid the price for sin on the cross, so the way is now open for us to know God and enjoy him forever, if only we will trust him.

But Jesus wouldn't have told the parable of the sower if that was an easy thing to do.

It's not something that will just happen regardless of whether or not we choose to act on what we hear.

The Sower himself is saying to you, "I can completely transform your life. But are you listening?"

8.
WHAT DO YOU WANT ME TO DO FOR YOU?

In Mark chapter 10, Jesus asks two of his followers – James and John – a very simple, but very revealing question:

What do you want me to do for you?

What it would be for you? Having explored who Jesus is and why he came, what would you ask Jesus for? What do you feel is your greatest want, your greatest need?

The brothers, James and John, know exactly what they want. But just before they tell Jesus what they want of him, Jesus tells them what he is about to do for them. And it is infinitely more valuable than anything they might have asked for:

"We are going up to Jerusalem," he said, "and the Son of Man will be betrayed to the chief priests and teachers of the law. They will condemn him to death and will hand him over to the Gentiles, who will mock him and spit on him, flog him and kill him. Three days later he will rise."

In other words, Jesus Christ, God's King in God's world, will deliberately go to Jerusalem, to be condemned in the capital city by the nation's leaders. As we've seen, he will deliberately give up his life for all those he came to save. Including James and John.

So, how will the brothers respond to the news that their Lord and Master, their closest friend of the past three years is about to be condemned, humiliated and killed?

> Then James and John... came to him. "Teacher," they
> said, "we want you to do for us whatever we ask."
> "What do you want me to do for you?" he asked.
> They replied, "Let one of us sit at your right and the
> other at your left in your glory." (Mark 10:35-37)

Paths of glory

Although they call Jesus "teacher", how much have they really understood?

He is deliberately going to Jerusalem, to give up his life for others. They, on the other hand, are desperately trying to cling on to their lives for themselves. While Jesus is serving others in the most costly way imaginable, they only want to be served by others. They want Jesus to give them power and prestige.

As we'll see, they still haven't understood why Jesus came or what it means to follow him. They don't yet see that Jesus' kingdom is only reached by a path that will take them (and us) through hardship and suffering and death. While Jesus is about to hang on a cross, they fantasise about sitting on a throne.

And this is not the first time the disciples have revealed a short-sighted lust for glory.

Three times in Mark's Gospel, Jesus tells his disciples that he must suffer, die and rise again. And the incredible thing is that on two occasions, the disciples' react by thinking only of their own greatness. They want power and prestige. They want importance and approval and recognition.

And if we have an eye for what is currently going on around us, we'll see the same lust for power just about everywhere we look. We see it in the medical profession, the legal profession, in sports, the arts, the world of politics and in big business. And, of course, we see it in church. It's very easy to convert the pulpit into a throne.

But Jesus wants something different for them, and for us. Something infinitely better.

> "You don't know what you are asking," Jesus said. "Can you drink the cup I drink or be baptized with the baptism I am baptized with?" (Mark 10:38)

"Drink the cup I drink" was a Jewish expression meaning to share someone's fate. So what Jesus means here is this: can you do what I will do? Can you die on behalf of sinners? Can you bring down the barrier separating sinful human beings from their Creator once and for all, so that they can have an infinitely satisfying relationship with God? And can you be raised to life again to prove that death and sin have been conquered? The brothers give an answer which goes some way to explaining why Jesus gave them the nickname "Sons of Thunder":

"We can," they answered. (Mark 10:39)

But of course, despite the bluster, they can't. Like you and me, James and John need to be saved themselves from God's rightful anger at sin, so how can they save others? As Jesus said, they don't know what they're asking.

Paths of suffering

And yet, in another way, the brothers spoke more truly than they knew. They would "drink the cup" that Jesus was about to drink. A few years later, long after Jesus' death and resurrection, James and John would both suffer as Jesus had. And Jesus already knew it:

> Jesus said to them, "You *will* drink the cup I drink and be baptized with the baptism I am baptized with..."
> (Mark 10:39, my italics)

But later, because they had both been witnesses of Jesus' death and resurrection, James and John would be transformed from selfish to selfless. They saw for themselves that the path to true glory, true power, true prestige – all of which they saw in the resurrected Jesus – passed through death. So they were transformed from men desperate to cling on to their lives for themselves, into men who would joyfully give them up for the sake of Jesus.

Rather than seeking their own glory, they would seek the glory of Jesus, knowing that glory is found in serving, rather than being served:

> Jesus called them together and said, "... Whoever wants to become great among you must be your servant, and

> whoever wants to be first must be slave of all. For even the
> Son of Man did not come to be served, but to serve, and
> to give his life as a ransom for many." (Mark 10:42-45)

James and John began by asking Jesus if they could take an exalted position, high above everyone else, one on his right and the other on his left. At the time, they had no idea that following Jesus involved suffering. But in a matter of weeks, their words would come back to haunt them, as two thieves were lifted up, high above everyone else, and crucified with Jesus, "one on his right and one on his left."[15] If we really want to take our place in glory alongside the one who came to serve rather than be served, the one who gave his life as a ransom for many, we must be prepared to take our place alongside him in suffering.

Too easily pleased

But why would anyone want to trade in status – or anything else – for suffering and service? How can we possibly loosen our grip on the things that we want so badly?

The reason James and John (and we, if we're being honest) grasp after these things is because we don't understand that Jesus is already offering us something infinitely more valuable. Himself.

If Jesus had simply given us what we wanted, it would never satisfy us anyway. No amount of power, or money, or achievement, or family, or friendship, or sex or spirituality is ever enough in itself. We just want more.

And there's a reason for that. The deepest cravings we

---

15 Mark 15:27

have – the ones that we unsuccessfully try to fill with all these other things – can only be fully satisfied by loving and serving the One who made us. It's the way He made us to be.

We go looking for contentment and satisfaction and fulfilment in all the wrong places, and we chase after them in the hope that they'll give us what only God can. In the Bible, it's called idolatry: turning something God has created into a substitute for God. Turning a good thing into a God thing.

And Jesus' closest disciples do it, even when Jesus has just personally offered them the greatest treasure in the entire universe.

The writer C. S. Lewis once said,

> We are half-hearted creatures, fooling about with drink
> and sex and ambition when infinite joy is offered us, like
> an ignorant child who wants to go on making mud pies in
> a slum because he cannot imagine what is meant by the
> offer of a holiday at the sea. We are far too easily pleased.

That's James and John. That's us. Far too easily pleased. If only we had eyes to see it.

But James and John aren't the only ones in this chapter who make a request of Jesus. Strikingly, Jesus asks that same question – "What do you want me to do for you?" – twice in Mark chapter 10. The second time he asks it, he asks it of a blind man called Bartimaeus.

Bartimaeus

> As Jesus and his disciples, together with a large crowd,
> were leaving the city, a blind man, Bartimaeus (that is,

> the Son of Timaeus), was sitting by the roadside begging.
> When he heard that it was Jesus of Nazareth, he began
> to shout, "Jesus, Son of David, have mercy on me!"
> (Mark 10:46-47)

Bartimaeus is different from the disciples in many ways. Apart from the fact of his physical blindness, he is a beggar who has nothing of material value apart from his cloak. He doesn't call Jesus "teacher", but "Son of David" – in other words, God's King in God's world. It's the only place in Mark's Gospel that we see someone recognize Jesus in this way.

And rather than coming to Jesus with a demand that Jesus should do for him whatever he asks, Bartimaeus knows he deserves nothing, has nothing to offer, and simply cries out for mercy.

> Many rebuked him and told him to be quiet, but he
> shouted all the more, "Son of David, have mercy on me!"
> (Mark 10:48)

Unlike the disciples who care about their own status, Bartimaeus is willing to make a fool of himself in the eyes of others, so long as he is able to get close to Jesus.

> Jesus stopped and said, "Call him."
> So they called to the blind man, "Cheer up! On your feet!
> He's calling you." Throwing his cloak aside, he jumped to
> his feet and came to Jesus. (Mark 10:49-50)

The cloak is all he has of any material value. But he lets it fall to the ground, because he knows that standing right in front of him there is something – or someone – of infinitely greater worth. I wonder what material desires you would be willing to throw aside, in order to come to Jesus?

And then Jesus asks him the same question he asked the brothers. How will Bartimaeus respond?

> "What do you want me to do for you?" Jesus asked him.
> The blind man said, "Rabbi, I want to see." (Mark 10:51)

The disciples wanted thrones, glory, power and prestige, but this man asks simply "to see". And that, ironically, is exactly the request James and John should have made.

> "Go," said Jesus, "your faith has healed you."
> Immediately he received his sight and followed Jesus
> along the road. (Mark 10:52)

While the brothers – despite their advantages – are spiritually blind, this beggar – despite his blindness – has clearly seen something they have not. While the disciples demand that Jesus do whatever they ask of him, Bartimaeus knows he's in no position to make demands. He knows his weakness, his blindness. He knows what he needs more than anything. He doesn't need status or power or prestige. He simply needs mercy. He simply needs to see.

And while the disciples are rebuked by Jesus for their request, Bartimaeus is "healed". In the original Greek, the word literally means "saved".

We may be tempted to think that it was easy for Bartimaeus to come to Jesus. After all, he had nothing to lose, unlike the disciples. (As Peter himself said, "We have left everything to follow you!"[16])

---

16 Mark 10:28

But actually, Bartimaeus had considerably more to lose than the disciples. Peter and the others could presumably have returned to their day jobs. But for Bartimaeus, the price of following Jesus was even more dramatic: to receive his sight meant giving up his livelihood as a blind beggar.

Becoming a servant of Christ always comes at a price. But what we gain is infinitely, unimaginably more precious than anything we may have to give up.

So what will you ask Jesus for? What do you want him to do for you?

9.
WE ARE THE CHOICES
WE HAVE MADE

What is it that determines the choices we make?

The May edition of *Men's Health* magazine promised that I could have a flat belly by summer. All I had to do was choose a different diet, and a carefully-tailored exercise regime.

Well, it's summer. By all accounts, I should already be what the magazine described as "a leaning tower of power". But as I look down, a more accurate description would be "a wobbling vat of fat." Sadly, my waistline resembles a family-size pack of marshmallows. (It's the old gag: "I now have a furniture problem: my chest is in my drawers." Which seems a lot less funny now than when I first heard it twenty years ago.)

I never before realized the complete truth of what Meryl Streep's character says in *The Bridges of Madison County*: "We are the choices we have made."

Herod chose to rebel

Mark chapter 6 contains one of the darkest moments in

RICO TICE | BARRY COOPER

the Bible. It records the story of King Herod Antipas, the ruler of Galilee, a man who tragically refused to make the right choice, even though it cost a man his life – and may well have cost him his own.

Also caught up in the tragedy is John the Baptist, a man we were introduced to at the very beginning of Mark's Gospel. A friendless, solitary figure, John the Baptist tells people about Jesus and the rescue he offers. He urges people to "repent", a word which means to turn away from sin, and turn back to God. And that's exactly the kind of talk that can get you into serious trouble.

> Herod... had given orders to have John arrested, and he had him bound and put in prison. He did this because of Herodias, his brother Philip's wife, whom he had married. For John had been saying to Herod, "It is not lawful for you to have your brother's wife." So Herodias nursed a grudge against John and wanted to kill him. But she was not able to, because Herod feared John and protected him, knowing him to be a righteous and holy man. When Herod heard John, he was greatly puzzled; yet he liked to listen to him. (Mark 6:17-20)

Before he met Herodias, Herod had been married for over twenty years. However, during a visit to Rome, he allowed himself to fall in love with Herodias, his brother's wife. Herod proposed to her and she agreed to leave her husband, as long as Herod agreed to leave his wife.

So they started living together in Galilee. And even though John the Baptist tells Herod that what he's doing is wrong, and we know that Herod respects John as a "righteous and holy man", Herod ignores the warning.

He puts John in prison, perhaps partly to protect him from Herodias, who wanted John dead because of what he'd been saying.

We're told that every time Herod heard John, he was "greatly puzzled". Now this doesn't mean that he was confused by John's teaching, as John's teaching was very clear. It means that Herod felt puzzled because his morals were thrown into confusion, as John exposed the way in which Herod was rebelling against God. Nevertheless, Herod "liked to listen to him."

Perhaps you've experienced a similar sense of puzzlement as you've come to see that you've been living life without reference to the loving Creator who made you. Perhaps, like Herod listening to John, you listen to the words of Jesus and want to go on listening, despite the disturbance they cause.

So Herod continued to listen. Week after week it went on. The people at the palace must have thought that their king had gone religious.

Mark tells us that "Herod feared John", to the extent that he even "protected him", but there was something that Herod was not prepared to do.

Herod chose not to repent

Yes, he would listen. Yes, he acknowledged that John was a just and holy man. Yes, he was even prepared to protect John. But Herod would not stop his adultery. He would not turn away from what he knew was wrong. Or as the Bible puts it, he would not repent.

As we've seen, the right response when we understand that we have been rebelling against God is to repent. It is to do an about-turn, to turn away from our rebellion and come to God for forgiveness and rescue. But that's the one thing Herod won't do.

Then one day, on his birthday, Herod throws a party for all his friends and colleagues. Mark's comment at this point is very striking: "Finally the opportune time came." As we're about to see, it's an opportune time for Herod, but also for Herodias. The question is: who will seize the opportunity, and who will miss it?

> On his birthday Herod gave a banquet for his high
> officials and military commanders and the leading men
> of Galilee. When the daughter of Herodias came in and
> danced, she pleased Herod and his dinner guests.
> (Mark 6:21-22)

During the banquet, Herodias's daughter Salome performs a dance which "pleased" Herod and his dinner guests. Put literally, she dances in a way that gets the half-drunk guests sexually aroused. Herod, in a phrase designed to impress upon his guests what a generous, powerful man he is, says to this teenage girl:

> Ask me for anything you want, and I'll give it to you."
> And he promised her with an oath, "Whatever you ask I
> will give you, up to half my kingdom." (Mark 6:22-23)

The girl immediately runs to her mother:

> She went out and said to her mother, "What shall I ask
> for?" (Mark 6:24)

It's "the opportune time" for Herodias, and she doesn't need to be asked twice. Back the girl runs to Herod:

> I want you to give me right now the head of John the
> Baptist on a platter. (Mark 6:25)

Herod is suddenly the only one not laughing in the banqueting hall. But this is the opportune time in Herod's life. He is suddenly in an extremely dangerous place.

We are the choices we make.

And this choice – this moment – will have a profound effect on what Herod will become. Will he stand up for what he knows is right, or will he once again do what he knows is wrong?

> The king was greatly distressed, but because of his oaths
> and his dinner guests, he did not want to refuse her. So
> he immediately sent an executioner with orders to bring
> John's head. The man went, beheaded John in the prison,
> and brought back his head on a platter. He presented it
> to the girl, and she gave it to her mother. (Mark 6:26-28)

Under pressure from friends, family and work colleagues, Herod allowed the head that warned him, the tongue that told him to repent and be rescued, to be literally cut off.

Much as he feared John, he feared his guests more. And when all is said and done, I wonder if Herod's guests really did respect him any the more for keeping his drunken oaths and needlessly slaughtering a man he had previously protected.

But how many of us would have done something similar in Herod's position? The fact remains that many, many people will do just that: at the opportune time, we will deny what we know is right because of what the family will think, what business colleagues may do, or because of what friends will say. Or because we know it will mean changing much-loved habits.

The cost

It's no small thing when we consider what we have to lose if we obey Jesus' words. Jesus himself knew first-hand what it felt like to suffer, to be misunderstood and ridiculed – even by his own family.

In Mark chapter 3, we read that his family "went to take charge of him, for they said, 'He is out of his mind.'" (Mark 3:21)

But when his family arrive at the house where he is teaching, Jesus says something remarkable.

> A crowd was sitting around him, and they told him, "Your mother and brothers are outside looking for you."
> "Who are my mother and my brothers?" he asked.
> Then he looked at those seated in a circle around him and said, "Here are my mother and my brothers! Whoever does God's will is my brother and sister and mother." (Mark 3:32-35)

It may be that in listening to Jesus, you feel afraid of what it will cost you to do what you know is right. I hope his words here are a great comfort to you. They're a great reminder that if you start to follow him – even if the people closest to you think you're out of your mind – there is a loving family of fellow believers who are there to support and encourage one another. Whoever does God's will, whoever follows Jesus, is your brother and sister and mother.

But it goes even further than that. In Mark chapter 10,

Jesus makes this amazing promise to all those who put their trust in him:

> "I tell you the truth," Jesus replied, "no one who has left home or brothers or sisters or mother or father or children or fields for me and the gospel will fail to receive a hundred times as much in this present age (homes, brothers, sisters, mothers, children and fields — and with them, persecutions) and in the age to come, eternal life." (Mark 10:29-30)

There will be persecutions and pain of one kind or another if we follow Jesus. But with them, Jesus promises extraordinary blessings, and extraordinary joy that will far, far outweigh any suffering we might face.

John the Baptist and Jesus

Herod's story suggests a comparison of John with Jesus. Both preached the same gospel: that we need to turn from our rebellion against God, and accept the rescue he has lovingly provided. Both were protected by powerful men – Herod and Pontius Pilate – men who both tried to remain neutral but could not. And both John and Jesus suffered violent deaths as a result.

There is, of course, one further point of comparison. Why were both John and Jesus killed? Because in both cases, when Herod and Pilate found themselves under pressure from those around them, they would not make what they knew was the right choice.

So what choices will we make? It's an important question because, although we are free to repent or not to repent, we are not free to determine the consequences of our actions.

Herod's story is horrific – not just because of the gory details, but because it shows that for those who repeatedly choose not to repent, it becomes increasingly less likely that they will ever do so. In Mark chapters 1 to 3, we see Jesus' awesome power and authority. In chapters 4 to 5, we see the power of his teaching and of his word. And yet, at the beginning of chapter 6, we see him rejected by his home town. Their familiarity with Jesus bred contempt, they take offence at him and they reject him. Jesus' response in subsequent chapters is to take his preaching elsewhere. He instructs his disciples to do likewise, saying that if people will not listen, they should move on. That's the pattern: the message will be rejected by some, who will themselves be rejected because of their response.

Herod and Jesus
Herod is mentioned a final time in the Gospels. Pontius Pilate sends Jesus to meet Herod, and in Luke chapter 23, Luke records what happened. The meeting between Herod and Jesus is ominous, not because of what is said, but because of what is not said. Luke tells us:

> When Herod saw Jesus, he was greatly pleased, because for a long time he had been wanting to see him. From what he had heard about him, he hoped to see him perform some miracle. He plied him with many questions, but Jesus gave him no answer. (Luke 23:8-9)

You see, there does come a time, after repeatedly refusing to repent, when sadly there is no longer an opportunity to do so. It's easy to put it off, to say that we don't have the time, to think that we have too much to lose, or that there'll be a more convenient time in the future.

Of course, it's never easy to repent. It's rarely convenient. But Herod's story reminds us that there is a cost when we refuse to listen to God's word. It also warns us that we may not get an opportunity later.

When Herod gets no answer from Jesus, he and his soldiers mock him by dressing Jesus in an elegant robe and sending him back to Pilate, who enjoys the joke.

We read that on that day, "Herod and Pilate became friends – before this they had been enemies."

It is a tragedy that John the Baptist lost his life. But the tragedy of Herod himself is even greater. Because when he silenced John, he lost something that was more precious even than life itself: the opportunity to turn away from his wrongdoing and turn back to God. The opportunity to repent.

We only have one life. If we spend it ignoring Jesus' call to repent and believe, it may earn us the approval of other people. It may even win us friends. But, as Herod discovered, it will eventually earn us the rejection of Jesus.

We are the choices we make.

10.
COME AND DIE AND LIVE

A little boy at Sunday School is asked to draw a picture of Mary, Joseph and the baby Jesus in the midst of their flight into Egypt. The teacher had been telling them about the time in Matthew chapter 2, when an angel appears to Joseph in a dream and warns him to flee with his family from the murderous King who wants to kill all the baby boys living in Bethlehem.

So the little boy carefully draws a picture of a huge aeroplane and when the teacher asks him what it is, he points out that it's "the flight into Egypt", indicating Joseph, Mary and the baby Jesus, who are sitting happily in the passenger seats. "But who's that?" asks the teacher, pointing to a shadowy figure in the cockpit. Growing a bit tired of all the stupid questions, the little boy says, "That's Pontius the Pilot, of course."

It's not only five year-olds who misunderstand what Christianity's about. There must be millions of people in the United Kingdom alone who have rejected what they think is Christianity, but who have in fact rejected a pale imitation of the real thing. There must also be a great many Christians who have lost sight of the basics.

So as we finish, I want to look at Mark chapter 8. In this chapter, we see Jesus explaining that a Christian is someone who knows who Jesus is, understands why he came, and is prepared to follow him – whatever the cost. In a way, Mark chapter 8 sums up everything we've explored so far.

Who is Jesus?
This question has dominated the book of Mark up to chapter 8 and we, the readers, already know the answer. As we've seen, Mark's given the game away in the very first verse, where he tells us that this is a book of good news about Jesus Christ, the Son of God. It's a bit like an Agatha Christie novel beginning with the words, "The butler did it." You might think it would drain the book of all interest, but the fact is that the disciples don't know what we know. And we follow them around, watching as they try to make sense of Jesus.

Jesus, for his part, forces them to ask questions about who he is by doing amazing things, as we've seen. They watch him calming a vicious storm, curing incurable illness, bringing a little girl back from the dead. They even hear him claiming to be able to forgive sin.

And yet they don't draw the obvious conclusion: that this is God's Anointed One, the Christ, the Son of God, the one who'd been promised throughout the Bible. They were expecting it, were desperately hoping for it, but now that he's there, standing right in front of them, they just don't see it.

Have you ever seen one of those "magic" pictures that seem to show one thing but – looked at another way – show something entirely different? The most well known of these images is probably the picture of a beautiful young woman that can also look like a hideous old hag.

I have to admit that, despite staring at that picture for a long time, it was ages before I could see the beautiful young woman. All I saw was the hideous old hag. And if you're an amateur psychologist, I'm sure you could have some fun with that.

But I wonder what you've seen as you've looked at the picture of Jesus in Mark's Gospel? Because in a similar way, as we look at Jesus, there are two aspects to his identity, two faces to be seen at the same time. There's the human face of Jesus, but there's also the divine face of Christ. And not everyone can see both.

Some of us, just like the disciples, can stare at the face of Jesus for years – and all we can see is the man. Like the disciples in Mark's Gospel, it's possible to spend lots of time in Jesus' company, and yet be totally blind to the divine face of Christ.

Well, what did the disciples see when they looked at him? They saw an apparently uneducated man who taught as no one had ever taught. They saw a man who cured incurable diseases. A man who could control nature with a word. A man who took the hand of a corpse and raised it to life. A man who demonstrated authority to forgive sin.

They saw him do all these things. They ask themselves in Mark chapter 4 "Who is this?". And yet incredibly, they are still blind to the answer that Jesus has been giving them all along. By the time we get to Mark chapter 8, Jesus is exasperated with them:

> Do you still not see or understand? Are your hearts hardened? Do you have eyes but fail to see, and ears but fail to hear?

If being a first-hand witness of all these staggering events is not enough to make them see who Jesus is, then what hope is there? Who can possibly cure that kind of blindness?

Immediately, as if to answer that question, Jesus gives a blind man his sight.

But this healing is unique. It's the only one that happens gradually:

> They came to Bethsaida, and some people brought a blind man and begged Jesus to touch him. He took the blind man by the hand and led him outside the village. When he had spat on the man's eyes and put his hands on him, Jesus asked, "Do you see anything?"
> He looked up and said, "I see people; they look like trees walking around."
> Once more Jesus put his hands on the man's eyes. Then his eyes were opened, his sight was restored, and he saw everything clearly. (Mark 8:22-25)

Just like the optical illusion. It's a reminder that sometimes, even when we think we can see, actually we can only see part of the picture.

And then we reach a turning point in Mark's Gospel. Will the disciples finally be able to see who Jesus is?

> Jesus and his disciples went on to the villages around
> Caesarea Philippi. On the way he asked them, "Who do
> people say I am?"
> They replied, "Some say John the Baptist; others say
> Elijah; and still others, one of the prophets."
> "But what about you?" he asked. "Who do you say I
> am?" (Mark 8:27-29)

Jesus suddenly asks them a very personal question here, and this is where it gets very personal for us too. Can we only see the human face of Jesus, or can we also see the divine face of Christ? Who do we say Jesus is? Teacher? Healer? Miracle Worker?

> Peter answered, "You are the Christ."

This word "Christ" has big implications. It means "God's only chosen King." It's a title of supreme authority. Peter is saying that Jesus is the ultimate King, the one promised in the Bible, the one who would rescue all those who put their trust in him.

Finally, Peter sees it.

Or does he?

> Jesus warned them not to tell anyone about him.
> (Mark 8:30)

You see, Jesus knows the disciples' blindness is only partly cured. Although they can see who he is, they don't yet see why he's come – or how they should respond.

That's why Jesus immediately begins to teach them more about himself. It's as if he's starting to correct their partial vision of why he came.

Why did Jesus come?

> He then began to teach them that the Son of Man must
> suffer many things and be rejected by the elders, chief
> priests and teachers of the law, and that he must be
> killed and after three days rise again. (Mark 8:31)

That's why Jesus came. He came to die and rise again. In fact, Jesus himself says he "must" die. He knows it's the only way sinful people like you and I can be brought back into relationship with our loving Creator.

And now we reach the next turning point in Mark's Gospel. Peter has understood who Jesus is, but will he understand why Jesus came?

> Peter took him aside and began to rebuke him. (Mark 8:32)

Again, it gets very personal for us here. Can we see not only who Jesus is, but also why Jesus came? Do we understand how serious our sin is, and how badly we need rescue? Or, like Peter, does the idea of Jesus' death fill us only with horror and disgust?

If so, Jesus has some very strong words for us:

> When Jesus turned and looked at his disciples, he
> rebuked Peter. "Get behind me, Satan!" he said. "You
> do not have in mind the things of God, but the things of
> men." (Mark 8:33)

If we have in mind the things of men, then Jesus' death on the cross seems pointless, tragic and weak. But seen in a different way, having in mind the things of God, there has never been a more powerful moment in all of human history.

On 13 January 1982, millions of television viewers watched as a balding, middle-aged man swam in the icy-cold water of a river in Washington D.C. Seven inches of snow had fallen that day. The water was so cold that the life expectancy of anyone in it was no more than a few minutes.

A helicopter quickly reached the scene and let down a rope to haul the man to safety. The viewers at home were amazed as the man grabbed hold of the rope twice, then quite deliberately let it go. Each time the rope was lowered to him, he had a chance of survival – but he chose to let it go. And – in front of millions of mesmerized viewers – the man eventually died. It seems like a futile and pointless death. But we need to see the broader picture.

Five minutes earlier, at 4.00 p.m., Air Florida flight 90, a Boeing 737 jetliner carrying 83 passengers and crew, departed from National Airport's main runway. However, the ice that had built up on the wings as it waited for take-off prevented it from gaining sufficient altitude. Traffic on the nearby 14th Street Bridge was heavy with commuters. The *Washington Post* newspaper described what happened next:

> With an awful metallic crack, a blue-and-white jet swept out of the swirling snow… smacked against one of the bridge's spans, sheared through five cars like a machete, ripped through 50 feet of guard rail and plunged nose first into the frozen Potomac River.

The survivors struggled in the freezing river amid ice chunks, debris, luggage, seat cushions and jet fuel.

A rescue helicopter arrived. Life vests were dropped, then a flotation ball.

The television cameras picked out a balding, middle-aged man, passing them on to the others. The helicopter then let down its rope. The man, who was a strong swimmer, swam as fast as he could to the rope, grabbed it, and gave it to somebody else who was then pulled to safety. This happened twice before – exhausted – the man drowned. When we have all the details in front of us, an apparently futile death is shown to be purposeful, daring and amazingly loving.

There are two ways of seeing the cross. We can see it from a human perspective, as a pathetic and needless death. Or we can see it from God's perspective, as our only means of rescue. Although we don't deserve anything apart from his condemnation, and although he did not need to rescue any of us, yet in his amazing love, Jesus humbled himself by coming to earth, becoming a man, and suffering and dying for the very people who had been rebelling against him all their lives. He died for sinners, taking the punishment we deserve, so that we could enjoy the relationship with God that we were created to enjoy. Forever.

Our lives, as well as our deaths, will be determined by the way in which we respond to what Jesus did on the cross.

But there is one more thing the disciples need to understand before they see can see everything clearly. Because it is not enough to see who Jesus is. It's not even enough to see why he came. Just like the disciples, we also need to see what Jesus demands of us.

How should we respond?

Return with me to Mark chapter 8 verses 34 to 37. Jesus has just rebuked Peter for having in mind "the things of men". He now calls the crowd to him and tells them what it means to follow him. So if you want to know how you should follow Jesus, these verses are addressed to you:

> Then he called the crowd to him along with his disciples and said: "If anyone would come after me, he must deny himself and take up his cross and follow me." (Mark 8:34)

The explorer Ernest Shackleton, when he was looking for people to go with him on his exploration of the Antarctic, reportedly placed an ad in a newspaper. It said simply:

> MEN WANTED FOR HAZARDOUS JOURNEY. LOW WAGES, BITTER COLD, LONG HOURS OF COMPLETE DARKNESS. SAFE RETURN DOUBTFUL. HONOUR AND RECOGNITION IN EVENT OF SUCCESS.

There is something of that in Jesus' call to each one of us. The message is: "Come and die." Following him will cost us a great deal: it may cost us in terms of relationships, careers, comfort; it may even – in some places – cost us our lives.

But there's a crucial difference between Shackleton's call, and Jesus' call. The difference is that if we respond to Jesus' call, there is no doubt about the final outcome.

All the way through Mark's Gospel, Jesus has demonstrated ultimate power and authority over everything – sin, sickness, nature, even death itself. He has shown time and again his love, his mercy, his grace – even to the most broken, rejected people.

We only have one life. But if we entrust it to Jesus, it is not a suicidal gesture. In fact, it's the complete opposite. Listen to what Jesus says next:

> For whoever wants to save his life will lose it, but whoever loses his life for me and for the gospel will save it. What good is it for a man to gain the whole world, yet forfeit his soul? Or what can a man give in exchange for his soul? If anyone is ashamed of me and my words in this adulterous and sinful generation, the Son of Man will be ashamed of him when he comes in his Father's glory with the holy angels. (Mark 8:35-38)

You see, not only does Jesus have ultimate authority over sin, sickness, nature and death, he also has ultimate authority over us. If we try to save our lives by rejecting Jesus, we will end up losing the very thing we're so desperate to hang on to. If we really want to save our lives, we must entrust them to Jesus. And, having explored Mark's Gospel for ourselves, we can do that knowing that we can trust him.

A true follower of Christ is someone who clearly sees what it will cost to follow him, but does it joyfully anyway, knowing that Jesus is worth infinitely more. Even more than friendship or family or career, even more than life itself.

What is given up is nothing compared to what is gained.

Listen to him

Immediately after this, in Mark chapter 9, some of the disciples witness something that once again demonstrates powerfully that Jesus can be trusted, that he is exactly who he says he is.

> After six days Jesus took Peter, James and John with him and led them up a high mountain, where they were all alone. There he was transfigured before them. His clothes became dazzling white, whiter than anyone in the world could bleach them. And there appeared before them Elijah and Moses, who were talking with Jesus.
> Then a cloud appeared and enveloped them, and a voice came from the cloud: "This is my Son, whom I love. Listen to him!" (Mark 9:2-4,7)

The words are an echo of the words spoken at the very beginning of Jesus' public life, when he was baptized by John the Baptist:

> As Jesus was coming up out of the water, he saw heaven being torn open and the Spirit descending on him like a dove. And a voice came from heaven: "You are my Son, whom I love; with you I am well pleased." (Mark 1:10-11)

On both occasions, God the Father tells us who Jesus is – "my Son, whom I love". But here in Mark chapter 9, God also tells us how we should respond:

> Listen to him! (Mark 9:7)

So as our journey through Mark's Gospel comes to an end, we're left with three questions. First, what do you see when you look at Jesus? Is he just a good man, or is he the Christ, the Son of God? Second, what do you see when you look at his death? Was it just a tragic waste of a young life, or is it a rescue, a "ransom for many"?

And finally, what do you see as you consider Jesus' call? Is it a call simply to come and die? Or can you see that because of his death and resurrection, Jesus is calling you to come and die – and live.

What next?

If you've become convinced of who Jesus is and what he came to do, and you understand what it will mean to follow him, what now? Jesus tells us:

> "The time has come," he said, "The kingdom of God is near. Repent and believe the good news!" (Mark 1:15)

"Repent" means to turn away from the direction we're currently facing, and turn back to God. It means we start living life to please him rather than continuing to rebel against him. "Believe" means believing that Jesus is who he says he is, and putting our trust in him as a result. It means being for what he is for, and against what he is against.

But this radical change is impossible apart from the Holy Spirit. As Jesus said to his disciples, "With man this is impossible, but not with God; all things are possible with God." (Mark 10:27). So ask God to transform you, making it possible for you to follow Jesus.

If you do begin following Jesus, you'll want to:

• connect with a good local church. You can find one using the "course finder" at www.christianityexplored. org.

• begin reading the Bible. Now you've explored Mark, why not read one of the other three gospels: Matthew, Luke or John?

• begin praying. Praying is simply talking to God, and you can speak freely using your own words at your own pace, because God understands the longings of your heart – even if your words are hesitant and uncertain.

- be baptized. Baptism is a way of identifying with Jesus and his people, so speak to the pastor or minister at your church about being baptized.
- You might also find the next section of this book helpful.

If you're not yet ready to follow Jesus, but you would like to keep exploring, take a look at www. christianityexplored.org. You'll find videos answering tough questions, real life stories, the full text of Mark's Gospel, and information about the Christianity Explored course – a relaxed and informal way to get to know more about Jesus.

11.
HELP ON THE JOURNEY

So far we've focused exclusively on the life of Jesus as recorded in Mark's Gospel. But at this point, I'd like to explore some other parts of the Bible. This is for the benefit of readers who have just begun to trust Jesus for themselves, as we look at four ways God provides for his people.

This section may also be helpful if following Jesus sounds impossible to you. You're right, it is – if we're trying to do it in our own strength. But God never makes demands of us without supplying the means to meet them.

Prayer

There's a tiny whitewashed church in a tumbleweed-strewn shanty town. Clint Eastwood rides into view and finds a cowering monk, dressed in a coarse brown robe and clutching his hands together prayerfully. He looks up at Clint with a mixture of expectation and cowardice. Our hero glares out at him from beneath his broad-brimmed hat.

He's about to ride out and give the bad guys a good kicking. "Can I come with you?" asks the monk. "Nope. It's dangerous, and you don't know how to use a gun." "But I really want to help!" And at this, Clint contemptuously spurs his horse into action and shouts back at him, "Well, I guess you can always pray."

This idea that prayer is a weak measure, employed by people who can't do anything practical to help, is a popular one. The assumption is that God will not answer. It's like that episode of The Simpsons, where Homer says, "Dear Lord, the gods have been good to me. As an offering, I present these milk and cookies. If you wish me to eat them instead, please give me no sign whatsoever. [Brief pause] Thy will be done." And then he scoffs the lot.

But for Christians, prayer is not ineffectual; it's extremely powerful. Not because of the person praying, but because of the person being prayed to.

Take – for example – the prayer the disciples pray in Acts chapter 4. They start their prayer like this:

> Sovereign Lord... you made the heaven and the earth and the sea, and everything in them.

At this point, things could not be much worse for them. Their leader is no longer with them and their two main spokesmen have just been interrogated by the highest religious authorities, who are determined to shut them up. Rightly, in the face of such fierce opposition, they pray together, and it is interesting to see who they address their prayer to: "Sovereign Lord".

In fact, their whole prayer goes on to remind us of

how irresistibly powerful this Sovereign Lord is. They pray to the one who "made the heaven and the earth and the sea, and everything in them". So he made the world we live in and all the people who populate it. By quoting from Scripture written hundreds of years previously, they remind themselves that this "Sovereign Lord" fully expects earthly powers to "gather together" and plot against him and his "Anointed One", but that this plotting is "in vain". They continue:

> Indeed Herod and Pontius Pilate met together with the Gentiles and the people of Israel in this city to conspire against your holy servant Jesus, whom you anointed.

In effect, they remind themselves – and us – that although the situation seems to be terribly dangerous, the Sovereign Lord has seen it all coming a mile off. God is so completely in control, in fact, that, "They did what your power and will had decided beforehand should happen."

That is not to say that God's enemies are puppets who have no choice but to disobey God. The Bible makes it clear that everyone has the choice to obey or to disobey. But the disciples' prayer here gives us a glimpse of just how futile it is to oppose God: "They did what your power and will had decided beforehand should happen." You have to be unimaginably powerful to have your enemies do your bidding, even as they seek to destroy you. But that is precisely the kind of God who hears Jesus' followers when they pray.

So in the face of powerful opposition it is vital to pray, knowing that you are praying to a God who is more powerful. Romans chapter 8 tells us that "in all things God works for the good of those who love him".

Now of course, our "good" may not be what we expect or want. Rather than removing us from a particular situation, God may instead choose to equip us to handle it better. Or he may bring something into our lives that may not seem – from our perspective – to be very good at all.

But in the case of the disciples in Acts chapter 4, God acts in a very visible way. They ask for his help to "speak your word with great boldness" in the face of the threats and opposition confronting them, and then we read of the result: "After they prayed, the place where they were meeting was shaken. And they were all filled with the Holy Spirit and spoke the word of God boldly." So when Christians pray they are talking to the Sovereign Lord who always acts powerfully, even if not always visibly.

But that's not all. As well as being "Sovereign Lord", God is also – if you're a Christian – your Father. In Matthew chapter 6, Jesus teaches his followers specifically how they should pray:

> This, then, is how you should pray:
> "Our Father in heaven, hallowed be your name..."

Perhaps the most striking thing here is that Jesus tells his followers to refer to God as "Our Father". This reflects the intimacy people can have with God because of the cross. Indeed, the word Jesus uses for "Father" is closer to our word "Daddy". To be on such intimate terms with God is a tremendous privilege. It means that Christians can speak to God as they might speak to a loving earthly father: to thank him, ask him for support or forgiveness, confide in him, pour out their hearts to him. And nothing is beyond his concern, as we see in Philippians chapter 4 verse 6:

> Do not be anxious about anything, but in everything,
> by prayer and petition, with thanksgiving, present your
> requests to God.

Talking to a person frankly and consistently deepens our relationship with them, and indeed our love for them. In the same way, Jesus teaches that prayer is one way in which Christians deepen their relationship with their Father.

It also teaches them to be increasingly dependent on God for all their needs. Of course, dependence on a human being can be a bad thing. Unlike an earthly father, however, God always has the power to do what is best for those who love him. As we've seen, nothing is beyond his control, or his concern.

Some people treat prayer like the fourth emergency service – after the police, the ambulance and the fire brigade. A friend of mine talks about this kind of person as a foxhole Christian. A crisis comes – be it an exam I'm under-prepared for, or a traffic jam when I'm late for a meeting – and I think to myself, well, there's nothing else for it, I'd better pray. But Jesus teaches that Christians shouldn't only call upon God when they're in trouble. Instead, they should pray constantly, just as he did.

Why should Christians pray all the time? Well, we've already seen that prayer teaches them dependence, deepens their relationship with God and allows them to call on God's power. But, in addition, Jesus teaches his followers that prayer enables them to resist temptation. Look at verse 38 of Mark chapter 14: "Watch and pray so that you will not fall into temptation. The spirit is willing, but the body is weak."

There were a couple of blokes in my rugby team who lived their lives without reference to God, but who nevertheless used to "cross" themselves as they ran on to the field. It was a little self-help formula they used: a quick, superstitious prayer to get them in the right frame of mind. But that's not what Christian prayer is about.

As we've seen, it is the privilege of constantly pouring out your heart to an all-powerful Father. The comedian Spike Milligan was asked if he ever prayed and he said, "Yes, I do pray desperately all the time, but I've no idea who I'm praying to." For Christians, this is no longer the case: they know exactly who they're praying to.

The church

I know that church is not a popular subject. But let me get one thing clear straight away. When the Bible talks about "the Church", it's not referring to a building or to an old-fashioned institution. It's simply referring to all those who have put their trust in Christ.

God intends followers of Christ to be a support to one another. Now, hang on to your hats, because I'm going to say something profound: human beings are influenced by those they spend time with. I don't suppose that comes as a surprise to you, but it is an easy truth to forget. And the Bible reminds Christians that the people they spend time with can have a positive or a negative influence on them. Spending time in the company of other people who are seeking to follow Christ is one of the ways in which God wants Christians to be encouraged and inspired. We read in Hebrews chapter 10:

> Let us not give up meeting together, as some are in the habit of doing, but let us encourage one another...

The writer knows that, without this mutual encouragement, it will be hard to persevere. So if you are a Christian, it's very important to find a church where the teaching is faithful to God's word, where the people you meet are eager to welcome and support you, where they reach out in love to those who don't know Jesus, and where you are able to serve others. Sadly, not every church you visit will do these things. So don't be afraid to keep looking until you find one that does.

Psalm 1 also reminds Christians that they will be influenced by those with whom they keep company, whether in the real world, or in a virtual, online world:

> Blessed is the man who does not walk in the counsel of the wicked or stand in the way of sinners or sit in the seat of mockers.

Notice the way in which the psalmist describes what the blessed man is not like. This "unblessed" man goes from walking, to standing, to sitting: he is gradually grinding to a halt. How does this happen? It begins simply by walking alongside "the wicked", listening to their "counsel", getting their advice and perspective on the world. If this carries on long enough, he'll begin to pick up their habits and attitudes for himself. Finally, he ends up sitting "in the seat of mockers" – not only participating in this way of life, but actually mocking those who don't.

As followers of Jesus, we must be lovingly involved in the lives of others. Psalm 1 is not an instruction to separate ourselves from people who don't share our point of view. But it does mean being mindful that other people (not to mention books, movies, music, television, websites and social networks) do not have a "neutral" effect on us. As Psalm 1 makes clear, we must be wise, careful and alert in the way we engage with them.

Likewise, look at Proverbs chapter 13 verse 20:

> He who walks with the wise grows wise, but a companion
> of fools suffers harm.

For the Christian, this means – among other things – that they must spend time in the company of other Christians.

And because God has now become their "Father", other Christians have become their brothers and sisters. Now you may be thinking, "Hang on, I've already got a brother/sister, and one's enough." But nevertheless, 1 Peter chapter 1 verse 24 tells Christian brothers and sisters that they should "love one another deeply, from the heart".

It's not easy to do this, of course. But when Christians remember that they've been forgiven so much themselves, they will be much more likely to forgive what is unlovable in others.

Here's a description of early Christians, as written by the philosopher Aristides in the second century:

> They walk in all humility and kindness, and falsehood is not
> found among them, and they love one another: and from

the widows they do not turn away their countenance: and
they rescue the orphan from him who does him violence:
and he who has gives to him who has not, without
grudging; and when they see the stranger they bring him
to their dwellings, and rejoice over him as over a true
brother; for they do not call brothers those who are after
the flesh, but those who are in the spirit and in God...[17]

Even in the very early days of the church, then, the mark
of authentic Christian living was the love that Christians
showed one another.

The church is described in the Bible as "the body of
Christ": it's the visible presence of Jesus Christ on earth
until the day he returns. So becoming a part of a local
church is the natural way that a Christian expresses his
or her "belonging" to Jesus.

The Holy Spirit

Consider this. At the end of Jesus' life here on earth,
after a succession of awe-inspiring miracles and the most
amazing teaching the world has ever heard, how many
followers do you think Jesus had attracted to himself?
According to Acts chapter 1 verse 15, about 120.

The surprising fact is that, despite his remarkable life,
very few people were following Christ at the end of
his time here on earth. However, read on beyond the
Gospels – to the book of Acts – and see what happens
after Jesus leaves his disciples. For some reason, his
influence becomes even more powerful and compelling

---

17 Aristides, *The Apology of Aristides on Behalf of the Christians*, ed. J. R. Har-
ris (New Jersey: Gorgias Press, 2004), p.49.

in his absence. Nine days after Jesus left them, even though opposition to his followers had become ever more violent, we read that in one day no fewer than 3,000 people joined that tiny group of 120. After that, Acts tells us that more and more people were added to their number on a daily basis. Something sudden and extraordinary must have happened soon after Jesus left his followers.

And in fact, Jesus had already predicted it. He'd told his disciples what they should expect once he'd gone:

> But I tell you the truth: It is for your good that I am going away. Unless I go away, the Counsellor will not come to you; but if I go, I will send him to you. (John 16:7)

It is this "Counsellor" who is responsible for the tremendous growth of the early church. Earlier, Jesus had already promised that the Counsellor – or "Spirit" – would come to live "in" those who follow him:

> If you love me, you will obey what I command. And I will ask the Father, and he will give you another Counsellor to be with you for ever – the Spirit of truth. The world cannot accept him, because it neither sees him nor knows him. But you know him, for he lives with you and will be in you. I will not leave you as orphans; I will come to you. (John 14:15-18)

It's a promise that still holds true today in the experience of every human being who begins following Christ: the Spirit will come to live "with you" and "in you". In fact, the Greek word translated here as "Counsellor" is *parakletos*, which described a pilot guiding a ship into port. It was also used to describe a friend comforting a bereaved person. Literally, the word means "one who is called alongside".

Notice, too, that Jesus talks about another Counsellor. In effect, he is saying that this Spirit will do for believers what he himself has done for them while on earth: advising them, teaching them, guiding them and so on. The Spirit who comes to live in Christians is the Spirit of Christ himself.

I could summarize quite simply what the Holy Spirit brings to the life of those who follow Christ: he brings conflict, but he also brings a supernatural calm. Let me explain what I mean. The conflict comes because the Spirit urges and empowers Christians to wage war against their sinful nature, as Galatians chapter 5 verses 16 to 17 makes clear:

> So I say, live by the Spirit, and you will not gratify the desires of the sinful nature. For the sinful nature desires what is contrary to the Spirit, and the Spirit what is contrary to the sinful nature. They are in conflict with each other, so that you do not do what you want.

In other words, although the Spirit makes Christians want to please God (in fact he makes them delight in doing so), the sinful nature continues to fight against that desire. This feeling of inner conflict is strangely comforting, however, because it confirms that the Spirit is real and at work.

So, there is conflict, but the Spirit also brings with him an unearthly calm. Boris Becker, the great German tennis player, once said:

I'd won Wimbledon twice before, once as the youngest
player. I was rich: I had all the material possessions I
could want – money, cars, women – everything. I know
this is a cliché. It's the old song of the movie and pop star
who committed suicide; they had everything yet they are
so unhappy. I had no inner peace.

The Bible says that the reason for Becker's lack of peace
is separation from the God who made him. But when a
person begins following Christ, they no longer feel that
separation. Indeed, because the Spirit now resides in that
person, God is with them forever. That presence provides
peace, described in Philippians chapter 4 as "the peace of
God, which transcends all understanding".

Paul writes in Romans chapter 8 that this peace comes
from a deep inner conviction that the follower of Christ
is one of "God's children", no longer separated from
him, and certain to be with him in heaven. For Christians
facing opposition, that assurance of eternal life is a very
precious thing.

The Holy Spirit is powerful – powerful enough to
actually change those who follow Christ. The first time
I can remember the Spirit changing me in this way was
when I was sixteen and had just become a Christian.
Rugby was central to my life (now, of course, it's only
very important indeed). My friend John had just got
into the first team at school, and I was so jealous that I
couldn't sleep.

One day, after a practice in which John had played
particularly well, my sense of jealousy and desperation
was such that I walked into a shed beside the pitch,
knelt down and said, "Lord Jesus, please take this

jealousy away." I'd like to say that at that point another boy burst into the shed to tell me that John had been dropped, but no. Instead, I had a sense of being changed from within.

Three weeks later (after John had in fact been dropped), he came up to me and thanked me for remaining on friendly terms when so many others had allowed their jealousy to affect the way they treated him. But I knew that it wasn't me who deserved the thanks. When I was a bit older, I read this in the Bible – it's from Ezekiel chapter 36 verse 26:

> I will give you a new heart and put a new spirit in you; I will remove from you your heart of stone and give you a heart of flesh. And I will put my Spirit in you and move you to follow my decrees and be careful to keep my laws.

Here Ezekiel anticipates what Jesus does for his followers when he gives them his Spirit. He knows that the Spirit will change their hearts, giving them the desire to obey laws that would otherwise seem too hard to obey. Like the law that tells us not to covet what our neighbour has, even if they have just made it into the first team.

Lastly, the Spirit who actually inspired Ezekiel to write those amazing words, over 500 years before Jesus had even been born, is the same Spirit who lives in Christians today. 2 Peter chapter 1 verses 20 and 21, says this about the way that the Spirit was involved in the writing of Scripture:

> Above all, you must understand that no prophecy of Scripture came about by the prophet's own interpretation. For prophecy never had its origin in the

> will of man, but men spoke from God as they were
> carried along by the Holy Spirit.

So there is an additional way in which the Spirit changes the minds of believers: he enables them to understand the very words he has inspired. No wonder the Bible is a closed book to many people. Without the Holy Spirit, even great minds struggle to make sense of it. But that is another way in which God provides for those who follow him. He sustains them through his word.

The Bible

C. S. Lewis, best known for writing *The Lion, the Witch and the Wardrobe*, emphasizes the importance of reading the Bible in his book *The Screwtape Letters* – an imaginary series of letters written by a senior devil to a junior devil.

Their aim is to cause a man who has just become a Christian to lose his new-found faith. The senior devil tells the junior devil to make sure that the man's life is dictated by "the streams of immediate sense experience"; in other words, get him to rely on his feelings. The devils know that when life gets hard for the man, he may feel that his faith isn't real.

The solution proposed by the book – and by the Bible – is for the man to reassure himself of his relationship with God by focusing not on feelings, but on the unchangeable promises God makes in Scripture.

The truths contained in the Bible are unchanged by our moods or our circumstances. No matter how followers of Christ feel when they face opposition, they can look to the Bible and be reminded of what they know to be true.

I don't know if you're a sports fan (good job getting this far if you're not), but think about how you feel when you watch your favourite team on TV. If you're watching a recording, and you already know the final score, your emotions are very different from those you feel if you're watching a game live.

So when, for instance, the Bible tells us in Romans chapter 14 verse 11 that one day everyone will acknowledge Christ as Lord, even his fiercest opponents, it makes all the difference. It means that even if the opposition seem to be winning, Christians can be sure of the ultimate outcome. As Jesus says to his disciples in Mark chapter 13 verse 23: "I have told you everything ahead of time." Having the Bible is like already knowing the final score.

Christians (and the churches they attend) should take the Scriptures very seriously indeed. If Jesus did so, then his followers should certainly do likewise – especially given that they will face persecution just as he did. Jesus emphasized that knowing what the Bible says is the only way we can be sure our thinking is correct: "Are you not in error because you do not know the Scriptures or the power of God?"[18]

Jesus, with all his power, authority and insight, certainly treated Scripture as the very words of God. In Mark chapter 7, for example, he explicitly refers to Scripture as "the word of God".

Jesus lived, of course, in the time "between the testaments": what we call the Old Testament was already in use, but the New Testament had yet to be written.

---

18 Mark 12:24

Nevertheless Jesus anticipated the writing of the New Testament, preparing for it by choosing, appointing and equipping twelve "apostles". They were men who had unparalleled access to Jesus and his teaching, and their authority is such that Jesus said of them, "He who listens to you listens to me; he who rejects you rejects me."[19]

The New Testament is made up entirely of documents written by these apostles or by those under the immediate direction of the apostles – the only exceptions being James and Jude, who were Jesus' own brothers.

In addition, Jesus tells the apostles in John chapter 14 verse 26 that they will be well equipped to record his words with accuracy:

> But the Counsellor, the Holy Spirit, whom the Father will send in my name, will teach you all things and will remind you of everything I have said to you.

So Jesus' endorsement of what we call the Bible is impressive.

Perhaps we shouldn't be surprised. 2 Timothy chapter 3 verse 16 says this: "All Scripture is God-breathed". Although 100 percent of the book we call the Bible was written down by human beings, every word was the product of God's inspiration.

In a Times article, Stephen Fry once sang the praises of the Bible, with its beguiling styles and stories. It's true, of course – the form and content of the Bible are beautiful. But T. S. Eliot, perhaps the most important writer of the twentieth century, didn't agree with this view of the Bible as simply a collection of great writing:

---

19 Luke 10:16

> Those who talk of the Bible as a 'monument of English prose' are merely admiring it as a monument over the grave of Christianity.

There will always be people who see the Bible in the same way that they see butterflies in a glass case: beautiful and dead. But, as Jesus says in John chapter 7 verse 17, "If anyone chooses to do God's will, he will find out whether my teaching comes from God." In other words, the proof of the pudding is in the eating: when we obey God's words, we see God's power working miraculously in our own lives. There's nothing dead about it.

My aim in writing this book has simply been to make people better acquainted with who Jesus is. But to be honest, there's no better way of becoming acquainted with Jesus than by reading the Bible. As Jesus himself says in John chapter 5 verse 39,

> These are the Scriptures that testify about me.

ACKNOWLEDGEMENTS

For a short book, *One life* took a surprisingly long time to finish. Over the course of nearly four years, it passed through any number of drafts, revisions and rethinks.

One life is a revised and updated version of the *Christianity Explored* paperback that was originally published in 2002.

Our grateful thanks go to all those who have read these various manuscripts, offering suggestions, criticism and encouragement. We want to acknowledge the significant contributions made by Ollie Balch, Tom Bible, Dr Andrea Clarke, Paul Clarke, Jon Daniel, Ed Dickenson, Alison Mitchell, Sophie Peace, Naomi Rosenberg, Tara Smith, Edwina Thompson and Tim Thornborough. In particular, the patience, dedication and intelligence of Sam Shammas have immeasurably enhanced each chapter.

There is something in this book to offend everyone. Some of it offends us, and we wrote it. But none of the people named above should be held responsible.

Rico Tice and Barry Cooper

thegoodbook
COMPANY

Thanks for reading this book. We hope you enjoyed it, and found it helpful.

Most people want to find answers to the big questions of life: Who are we? Why are we here? How should we live? But for many valid reasons we are often unable to find the time or the right space to think positively and carefully about them.

Perhaps you have questions that you need an answer for. Perhaps you have met Christians who have seemed unsympathetic or incomprehensible. Or maybe you are someone who has grown up believing, but need help to make things a little clearer.

At The Good Book Company, we're passionate about producing materials that help people of all ages and stages understand the heart of the Christian message, which is found in the pages of the Bible.

Whoever you are, and wherever you are at when it comes to these big questions, we hope we can help. As a publisher we want to help you look at the good book that is the Bible because we're convinced that as we meet the person who stands at its heart—Jesus Christ—we find the clearest answers to our biggest questions.

Visit our website to discover the range of books, videos and other resources we produce, or visit our partner site www.christianityexplored.org for a clear explanation of who Jesus is and why he came.

Thanks again for reading,

Your friends at The Good Book Company

thegoodbook.com | thegoodbook.co.uk
thegoodbook.com.au | thegoodbook.co.nz | thegoodbook.co.in

WWW.CHRISTIANITYEXPLORED.ORG
Our partner site is a great place to explore the Christian faith, with powerful testimonies and answers to difficult questions.